Daily
Enlightenments

G.S. Herrman

About the Author

Nathalie W. Herrman is a personal trainer, massage therapist, motivational speaker, and Reiki master. She graduated Magna Cum Laude from Boston University and has spent her life accumulating experience in the pursuit of optimal health and wellness in herself and others. Visit her online at NathalieWHerrman.com and enlightenmentdaily.blogspot.com.

Daily Enlightenments

365 Days of Spiritual Reflection

NATHALIE W. HERRMAN

Llewellyn Publications
Woodbury, Minnesota

FIRST EDITION
Third Printing, 2015

Book design by Donna Burch
Cover art: 13413769/iStockphoto.com/seraficus
Cover design by Ellen Lawson
Editing by Andrea Neff
Interior model(s) and photos are used for illustrative purposes only and may not endorse or represent the book's subject matter.
List of photo credits on page 385

Llewellyn Publications is a registered trademark of Llewellyn Worldwide Ltd.

Library of Congress Cataloging-in-Publication Data
Herrman, Nathalie W.
 Daily enlightenments : 365 days of spiritual reflection / by Nathalie W. Herrman. — First Edition.
    pages   cm
  Includes index.
  ISBN 978-0-7387-3712-6
1. Spirituality. 2. Spiritual life. 3. Devotional calendars. I. Title.
  BL624.2.H47 2014
  204'.32—dc23
                                                   2013038922

Llewellyn Worldwide Ltd. does not participate in, endorse, or have any authority or responsibility concerning private business transactions between our authors and the public.
  All mail addressed to the author is forwarded, but the publisher cannot, unless specifically instructed by the author, give out an address or phone number.
  Any Internet references contained in this work are current at publication time, but the publisher cannot guarantee that a specific location will continue to be maintained. Please refer to the publisher's website for links to authors' websites and other sources.

Llewellyn Publications
A Division of Llewellyn Worldwide Ltd.
2143 Wooddale Drive
Woodbury, MN 55125-2989
www.llewellyn.com

Printed in the United States of America

Dedicated to Love

$\mathcal{A}$cknowledgments

Let us rise up and be thankful.
—BUDDHA

I would like to thank Angela Wix and her colleagues at Llewellyn for believing in this book and making it a reality; my loving husband, Gruff, for his unending patience and support; my parents, Blair and Reuel, for the opportunities they've given me; and my children, Sienna and Nick, for blessing my life.

I would also like to thank the models of the photographs and the contributing photographers whose images ground my words. In particular, I would like to thank Stuart Rakoff, Jeff Bingham, Kimberley Berlin, and Mike Florio. This book would not be what it is without their exceptional and beautiful way of seeing the world!

I want to thank my clients and friends as well, and to express my gratitude for good health, a love of words, and the ongoing willingness to pursue this work. And finally, I would like to thank my readers. None of this means anything without you.

Contents

$\mathcal{I}$ntroduction

Ever since I was a girl, I have been interested in spirituality. When I first heard about the idea of "enlightenment," it was something I wanted, and I set off to find it. Over the years, I tried pendulums, oracle cards, numerology, shamanic journeying, sweat lodges, past-life regressions, hypnosis, yoga, methods of meditating, and you name it. I was rather a metaphysical junkie. And then one day, in a moment of presence, it occurred to me that perhaps enlightenment wasn't something to be achieved or sought after at all, but was easily accessible, and available to me at any and all times.

Like all of us, I have had my share of hardships. I've been married and divorced. I've raised children alone and buried a sister. I've experienced all kinds of personal trauma and engaged in self-destructive habits. I've drowned my sorrows in alcohol and ice cream. I've tried and failed at endless ventures. And through it all, I have learned lessons and been willing to change and to grow. I have learned to be self-reflective, and I have learned what helps and what doesn't.

I am a massage therapist and personal trainer by trade, and I love people. I love working with them, and I love to hear their stories. I see their beauty and feel their pain. I love to share my stories with them as well, and share the things that I have learned and all of the simple tools for better living that I have encountered.

I believe without a doubt that we are spiritual beings, but that we lose track of our divine essence as we try to keep up with the rigorous demands and responsibilities of life. We fall victim to the "tyranny of the urgent" and forget who we really are and what really matters. We worry and fret and try to control outcomes and manipulate people and situations in an effort to feel safe and secure in our lives. We rush around, moving ever faster, and we have become pretty good at doing multiple things at once. What we are not so good at is slowing down and enjoying the simple pleasures of life, of savoring our days and our families and friendships and taking good care of ourselves.

I have learned that if we can take five minutes at the beginning of our day, perhaps while drinking coffee or eating breakfast, or maybe in the car before our first appointment ... if we can learn to ground ourselves for just a moment in some kind of spiritual truth, then I believe we can improve the quality of our lives. This book is a tool to help us do that. It has helped me in the writing of it, and it is my hope that it will help you in the reading of it.

Daily Enlightenments are practical in their application and full of useful ideas for better living. They are for those who want to bring higher consciousness to the way they do things. Each entry is a reminder: to make better choices, to pause, to question our limiting beliefs, to grow, to believe in what's possible and celebrate our intrinsic worth as living beings, to stop worrying, and to follow our dreams.

Each entry concludes with a summary affirmation to take away. You might write it down or repeat it to yourself silently throughout the day. In order to best apply the spiritual concept of the daily reading to the actuality of your life, I suggest that you carry the ending affirmation with you somehow, if only as an echoing reminder in the back of your mind.

Everything I know I have learned from others and from life experience, and I am grateful for the opportunity to share some of it in this book. My hope and prayer is that these pages will be useful and that you will discover tools within them to improve your life.

January 1

Your heart is full of fertile seeds, waiting to sprout.
—MORIHEI UESHIBA

I love fresh starts. I love the way our cyclical life works. I love that our emotional and physical slates are swept clean every night when we sleep, so that every morning we have an opportunity to do things differently and to see and experience our lives differently. And if we add to that the adventure of a whole new calendar year, we are doubly blessed with fresh-start opportunity.

Let's celebrate the new year! Let's commit to better behavior and more mindfulness. Let's remember that meaningful change takes time to integrate, and that if one day or one situation doesn't go exactly the way we think it needs to, we don't have to throw up our hands and give up on the whole journey. Let's not cop out on ourselves. As many times as we fumble, let's pick ourselves up. Let's start over and over, as many times as it takes.

Every day is a fresh start. I can change the way I see things,
and the way I react, and the way I treat myself and others.
I can live better every day that I live.

January 2

Your assumptions are your windows on the world.
Scrub them off every once in a while, or the light won't come in.
—ALAN ALDA

We build our lives on assumptions. We assume that we will maintain our current state of health; that certain people can be trusted and that others cannot; that our parents will predecease us and that our children will make intelligent life decisions. If we are honest, we can peer into our reality and see how strongly we are rooted in all that we assume.

But when our belief system is crushed by life circumstances and we are driven to question everything we have ever believed, how do we handle it? Anything can happen to any of us at any time. The reality of that fact is what makes for an interesting life adventure and is where all great stories begin. So rather than railing against our assumptions when they crumble, let's fill ourselves with wonder and curiosity. Let's see how unfamiliar territory that we never knew existed is suddenly open to us, and enthusiastically embrace the burgeoning new frontier.

I am willing to let my long-held assumptions
dissolve when the time is ripe.

January 3

Respect yourself and others will respect you.
—CONFUCIUS

Are we able to be our own best friend? Or are we more usually our own worst enemy? Are we crueler and harsher with ourselves than we would ever consider being with other people, and do we feel like that's pretty much what we deserve? Is it the last thing we think of to forgive our mistakes? Do we habitually chastise ourselves and think that we should have known better, we should have done better, and we should really *be* better in every way?

Just because that's what we do and have always done doesn't mean it's what we have to continue to do. Let's take a risk and celebrate the wonder of who we are, every day, in every way. Let's be willing to try things and explore our gifts and talents. Let's figure that we're here for a reason and that we must have something to contribute. Let's share a smile and spread a little joy and look for the good everywhere we turn. Let's like ourselves for a change and give ourselves the break that we deserve.

I stop belittling myself and creating self-sabotage at every turn.
I make an effort to be my own best friend.

January 4

Don't underestimate the value of Doing Nothing.
—A. A. MILNE

Here's the antidote to doubt and feeling overwhelmed: stop everything and regroup. That's the answer to discombobulation, sloppiness, agitation, and exhaustion as well. So often we push on and on, beyond reason, beyond sense, in some kind of stubborn exertion of rigid willpower. But all of our answers and our relief come from stopping—not from pushing on and not from slowing down, but from the cessation of all movement.

Then, once we have gathered ourselves, we can begin again, slowly, and with calm. It may take an hour, or a few days, or longer. We will know when we are ready to know. We keep things simple as long as it takes and wait for life to loosen, and for elements of the confusion to equalize, and clarify, and open the path for our next right step. And when we see it, then we take it, and we go on from there.

When I am frazzled and frustrated,
I stop, and wait, for calm and clarity to return.

January 5

Savor the mystery.
—David McCallum

As a culture, we have a kind of grabbing and gulping mentality. We do more than eat on the run. We live on the run. We overstuff our hours as well as our bellies. We lack quiet time and reflection. We lack appreciation for all of the things we rush through to get to the next thing. We ache with impatience. No matter how much we have, we cannot get our fill. We want and want and want. And when we receive what really matters, we don't recognize it. Grabbing at life, we often miss the things that come to us as blessings and salvation. Our attention is elsewhere. We miss flavors and textures and the pleasures of slow digestion.

Let's back off and ease up. Let's savor each small step along the path and notice what's there. Let's taste and smell and see and hear with awareness and appreciation. This is the secret to pleasure: not *more* of anything, not fuller days or bigger bank accounts, but simply presence, and being who we are.

I stop rushing and savor my life.

January 6

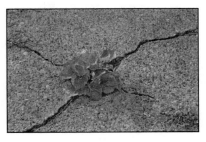

To the stars through difficulties.
—SENECA

We are incredibly adaptive. Things happen that seem impossible to integrate, that we are sure will hurt forever, or that we'll never find a way to live through, or with ... and yet we do. Over time, we learn to accommodate pain and scars, and more money and less money, and abusive people, and death and birth. Our experiences become a part of us. We absorb them.

And if we are conscious enough to do it, we can use absolutely everything that happens to us to enrich our life experience and enlarge our spirit. We can become wiser and more evolved. We can transmute suffering into growth. And in that may lie the key to our purpose here on earth: to experience the happenings of our lives and to learn something from each of them every step along the way.

I let everything that happens in my life serve me somehow.
I grow through difficulty.

January 7

You are imperfect, permanently and inevitably flawed.
And you are beautiful.
—Amy Bloom

What if we don't need to be more or less of anything to be perfect and beautiful? What if we are already perfect and beautiful just the way we are? And if that's true, what if we spend our whole lives measuring ourselves against impossible and impractical standards trying to determine our self-worth? And criticize ourselves for everything imaginable? And feel some level of loathing and contempt for our beings and our bodies, and a strong internal sense of not deserving love or reward or appreciation until we somehow prove ourselves? What if we spend our whole lives trying to prove ourselves? And use up all of our time and money and energy trying to fix all the things that ail us? What a lot of effort. We're all familiar with trying to fix ourselves.

But what if we're not broken? What if we're not really broken at all? What then?

I am willing to reconsider the way I feel about myself
in light of the possibility that I am already whole.

January 8

Between saying and doing, many a pair of shoes is worn out.
—ITALIAN PROVERB

Sometimes in life we have great vision and feel certain that we know exactly what we have to do and how perfectly our idea will work out. We start with the best of intentions and great gusto, but so many of our wonderful ideas fall flat in the end. Our lives are littered with abandoned exercise equipment, and unread books, and clothes that we have never worn. Perhaps we would do better with a little more waiting and seeing and a little less impulsive knowing.

Out of sheer eagerness, we tend to commit before we know what we're committing to, or whether it even suits us. People get married to each other in just this way, and accept jobs, and agree to all kinds of insanity. We want to arrive before we *actually* arrive, hoping for some kind of assured security, which is silly, perhaps, but frequent and common behavior nonetheless. We would rather force an outcome than agree to travel the road for a little bit and see how it feels.

> *I stop making impulsive decisions that affect my life and my wallet. I am willing to pause before leaping.*

January 9

It's not hard to make decisions when you know what your values are.
—ROY DISNEY

A friend of mine once told me to imagine a table between me and anyone with whom I am communicating. I find this especially helpful when the conversation is emotionally charged and potentially heated. Whatever is said to me lands on this imaginary table, and I can look at it lying there and consider it before I make a decision about how to respond.

I can pick up what is said to me and fling it back, or pick it up and consume it, choking on the words as I swallow them down. I can play with it, roll it over in my hands, or rearrange it and put it back on the table. I can throw it away. Or, I can just let it sit there. I don't have to pick it up at all. I can finish the conversation and walk away and leave it lying there, right where it landed.

The thing for me to remember is that what I do with whatever is said to me is my choice. I don't have to be hurt by hurtful words.

**Just because somebody says something about me,
or to me, does not make it a fact.**

January 10

*The only man I know who behaves sensibly is my tailor; he takes my
measurements anew every time he sees me. The rest go on with their old
measurements and expect me to fit them.*

—GEORGE BERNARD SHAW

When my children were born, they were six weeks early, which is
not unusual for twins. It made me nervous to bathe them because
they were so tiny. I remember them at every age—five, six, ten, thir-
teen—and now they are young adults. They are intelligent, strong,
and capable. They sit at the dinner table and share their philosophi-
cal insights, their triumphs, their sorrows, and their dreams. Somehow they went from being tiny infants in my arms to full-grown
adults, and I never actually saw them change. It just happened.

Everything in life is like that. The changes are too subtle to
witness while they are happening, and yet they are happening all
the same, in ourselves and in others. Evolution is always at work.

***I accept change as a slow process where nothing seems to be
happening. I keep on moving steadily in the direction I want to go,
and before I know it, I find myself already there.***

January 11

*A firm foundation is necessary for any building, institution,
or individual to endure.*
—Elder Russell M. Nelson

What is the condition of our foundation? Are our lives built on sand or stone? Are we rooted in God? In health? In how much we own? Are we living vicariously through someone else? Do we know who we are and what we value? Are we true to ourselves? Or do we live a lie? Do we live many lies?

Do we live in fear? Do we believe in scarcity, or abundance? In guilt and shame, or love and forgiveness? Are we friendly? Cheerful? Loving? Tolerant? Are we negative? Dark? Critical? Are we snobs? Do we live well? Sleep well? Act rightly? How could we improve our lives?

Our foundations matter. It is from our foundations that we rise. Are we solid and strong, or do we need to shore up and do some rebuilding?

*I consider in what soil I am grounded, and make changes
where changes are needed .*

January 12

Banish the ego ... You will then experience bliss.
—Sri Sathya Sai Baba

When we see through ego eyes, we are impressed by appearances and external shows of power and beauty. We are blind to the truth that lingers further back and can only be seen with the heart and the gut. We think we know what matters and who cares. We imagine ourselves far more important than we are in all the wrong ways and totally miss our *actual* importance as living spirits with deep, intuitive wisdom and endless love and compassion to share with the world.

But if we pay attention, we can learn to recognize the ego in action, and understand its agenda so as not to be blindly manipulated by its cagey charms. And we can learn to stay longer in truth and authenticity. If we care to take the time and do the work, we can live beyond the ego, and above it. We can find our way to be free.

*I get hooked by my ego. But I can disentangle
and learn to better recognize the bait.*

January 13

Better to light a candle than to curse the darkness.
—CHINESE PROVERB

It's interesting in life how we can be going along happily, merrily almost, and then, without warning, there is a shift within. We are suddenly dark and broody, as if we have been crossed, but it's hard to identify what or who has crossed us. We are so easily triggered, especially when we are tired and hungry. The slightest word uttered by someone we encounter can unleash a flood of old emotions and self-pity, and angst of every kind. And then we are subjected to the thrashing disorder of our feelings as they act out on us.

It's hard work being human. So many small things so easily become a big deal if we are not vigilant and aware of the flowing emotional currents inside of us. The path to peace is through awareness and attendance—watching ourselves and taking the time to diligently address our issues before they take over our day.

I bring awareness to the things in life that trigger my dark emotions and get a handle on them before they get a handle on me.

January 14

Make somebody happy today, and mind your own business.
—ANN LANDERS

We have ideas about what people *should* be doing and *how* they should be doing it, especially the people we love the most. If they are on a path we don't approve of, or are approaching their challenges in a way that doesn't make sense to us, we want to steer them right; and if they don't appreciate our suggestions, then feelings of resentment and bitterness creep into our hearts.

The only relief available is to drop our judgments. It's not our job to manage anyone else's life or to tell others how to go about things. We need to back off and trust them to find their way.

People don't behave according to our expectations or time frames. And if we keep on wanting them to do so, we will suffer greatly. Let's mind our own business and leave others to mind theirs. Our happiness doesn't depend on those around us behaving the way we want them to. It is the result of knowing what is ours to worry about and what is not.

I let the people I love find their way in life without my meddling and interference. I give them the freedom and respect to be who they are.

January 15

The soul has no gender.
—CLARISSA PINKOLA ESTES

No matter what kind of parents we have, we learn our gender roles from them. Unbeknownst to most of us, a deep-rooted belief system operates within us at all times, and we accept it as being true without even questioning it. If we make a list on paper of the roles and characteristics that we identify with men and with women, we may be surprised and enlightened. It may explain feelings we have, and potential resentments. Inevitably, the list comes from our youth, and is based on the way our mother and father behaved and how they acted toward and around each other. But just because it's what we grew up with does not mean it has to be what *we* live with, and die with.

Perhaps, if we're honest, our list could use some revision.

I take a moment to consider the beliefs I hold
about gender roles, and I am willing to change my mind
about my beliefs if they are sorely outdated.

January 16

A person often meets his destiny on the road he took to avoid it.
—JEAN DE LA FONTAINE

Our plans are skeletal at best. It is up to some power beyond us to fill them in with flesh and muscle. Call it God, or fate, or the universe, or whatever you wish, but this is the force that determines the experience. We cannot begin to foresee what obstacles we might encounter, or what inspiration may come our way.

Perhaps we hit a roadblock, or something unexpected tempts us to go in a different direction. We fall in love. We suddenly become ill. We hit traffic, have an accident, or otherwise lose our momentum. Every time our plan is foiled, we suffer. We feel stopped in our tracks, frustrated. But we need not. We can embrace any sudden change in anticipated speed or direction, understanding that a correction is being made; that there is some other plan beyond *our* plan that is meant for us; that there is somewhere else we are supposed to be.

I make plans, but remain flexible. Changes in direction are inevitable and serve a purpose beyond my understanding.

19

January 17

Touch is a life-giving thing.
—Robert Brault

Behind true gentleness there is power. It is the *restraint* of power and the *choice* to be soft that makes it feel nurturing to the recipient. It is firm, and strong even, but harsh in no way. It is touch filled with tenderness and a vast reservoir of loving kindness.

The dead fish touch, on the other hand, may be an attempt at gentleness, but comes across with a distinct element of creep instead. It tries to be gentle, but is so soft that it feels excruciating.

So it turns out that gentle is not what I have unconsciously supposed it to be for all these years. It is not soft, not really. It is strength instead. It is strength that has been generously subdued and voluntarily offered, in trust, in kindness, and in love.

I appreciate genuine gentleness and recognize that there's more to it than initially meets the eye.

January 18

You have to give it away in order to keep it.
—BILL WILSON

We are all longing for approval. We want to be loved. We want to be encouraged. We want to be thanked. Even if we don't admit it to ourselves, we want these things. We might pretend that we need no one and are just fine, thank you, and don't care a lick about what anyone thinks of us. But we all care a little. We can't help but care a little.

Sideways and backwards we go about getting these things. We try to demand them or bully others into giving them to us. Or else we become cynical, or whiny, and try to get what we need from a negative angle. The results of such attempts are dubious at best. The only legitimate way to receive love and appreciation is to give them to others. It's one of life's paradoxes. We get what we give.

> *I spread love and kindness because that's what*
> *I want to experience in my life.*

January 19

We turn not older with years but newer every day.
—EMILY DICKINSON

Youth is overrated. What pain and suffering we go through in middle school and high school! What angst we feel in puberty, and learning about love with all of its attendant heartaches and dependencies! And what upset comes from our greenhorn bravado as young adults taking the world by storm.

If we are open to it, aging comes with increased graciousness, wisdom, and calm. We know who we are and what we value. We know which foods and exercises serve our bodies best, and what and whom we love the most. I believe that life begins at forty, and then again at sixty, and then again at eighty. The longer we live, the more comfortable we can become with being in our own skin, and with how life works ... and doesn't work. We don't have to freak out over every little thing the way we did when we were sixteen, or thirty. I think growing old is a gift, not a burden. It is only horrible if that's the way we make it.

Every day that I live is an opportunity for good living.

January 20

Let things flow naturally forward in whatever way they like.
—LAO TZU

When we are frustrated trying to accomplish something in life, it's a natural inclination to expend extra effort. We think our lack of success must mean that we are not trying hard enough, that we have to do more, push harder, and somehow force the outcome with the strength of our will and muscle. But often, what is actually needed is *less* effort, and more flow, more surrender and rhythm and instinct. Whether it's hitting a golf ball, or playing soccer, or trying to get pregnant, or writing a novel, or proving a point, if we can relax and let go, we can release enough pressure to allow for grace and shifting movement.

It's obsessive wanting and insisting that create the pressure that gets us stuck in the first place. And it is difficult to accomplish things by force. If it's not happening, we need to leave it alone. We need to back off and get out of the way.

I catch myself in the energetic struggle of trying too hard to get something done that doesn't seem to want to get done. I am willing to back off and let go.

January 21

It's choice—not chance—that determines your destiny.
—JEAN NIDETCH

Thinking that we need to control everything is dangerous business; that if we don't do it, it won't get done right or won't get done at all. Such an attitude is a breeding ground for misery.

The kind of thought process we allow to motivate us is important. Are we driven by guilt? By a cheerful desire to be helpful? By greed? By fear? By martyrdom? We feel obligated to do certain things in our lives, but the truth is that it's *all* a choice. We think we "have to," but we don't. *Everything* is a choice. Everything. In what spirit do we choose? It's worth considering.

If we are hoping for peaceful living, we need to find the "want to" energy in our daily activities. Otherwise, we are nothing but victims, or sacrificial lambs, and we needn't be either. It's a waste of our time and our lives.

I'm honest about the energy that motivates me, and if it's dark energy, I am willing to change. Life is too short to be miserable.

January 22

We would rather be ruined than changed.
—W. H. AUDEN

As we change, our tastes change: our taste in clothes, music, books, people, exercise, food, and beauty—our taste in everything. And yet we have mental mindsets that lock in and stubbornly refuse to make the adjustments. We insist that we like something because we have always liked it. Maybe we associate it with pleasant memories from the past, or it served some purpose in our lives that we no longer need to serve. And maybe we don't really even like it anymore, but we keep on with it for old times' sake.

We do things because we have always done them. Giving up the familiar seems a high price to pay, and we resist. But the irony is that if we made the appropriate changes in honor of our changing bodies and spirits, we might actually *feel* better. In fact, we most certainly would. And it's possible, and maybe even likely, that contrary to our insistence otherwise, we might not actually end up missing the old stuff at all.

I am willing to give up the things in my life that I have outgrown.

January 23

Resentment is one burden that is incompatible with your success.
—DAN ZADRA

The most difficult people in my life have been my greatest teachers. They have taught me patience and acceptance. They have taught me compassion and forgiveness and how to hold my tongue. I used to feel anger. I had an instinctual desire for righteous retribution. But none of my angst has ever changed anything in other people. It has only made *me* unhappy.

I have come to understand that although some people are naturally fountains of love, others are not. Many times I have shown up at an empty well hoping to have my cup filled, and walked away disappointed. But I'm getting better about it. I'm starting to understand and be able to recognize who's who. I am learning to better accept people as they are, and not feel angry the way I once did. I can feel gratitude for the difficult people in my life today instead of resentment. Their dysfunction can work to my advantage if I only look at it the right way.

I am grateful for the difficult people in my life.
They teach me lessons that serve me well.

January 24

Addiction is just a way of trying to get at something else.
Something bigger. Call it transcendence if you want.
—TESS CALLAHAN

My favorite definition of addiction is "anything we hide." If that is the case, then what are we addicted to? It's interesting to watch ourselves jump to defenses as we consider our harmless "sneaks." Surely these aren't addictions, all the little rewards we give ourselves in secret: the snacks, the naps, the shopping adventures—whatever they may be. Why do we feel the need to hide at all? That's the deeper question. Why the longing for "secret" pleasures? Is it guilt that runs us over? Have we been programmed to believe that we don't really *deserve* treats and goodness and pleasure?

But what if we do? What if we really *are* deserving? Wouldn't it be liberating to not have to sneak around? Maybe we can find a way to stand tall and be okay with who we are and how we are, with all of our likes and dislikes—no apologies and no excuses. This kind of freedom is worth an awful lot, it seems to me. Maybe we ought to give it a try.

I don't apologize for who I am.

January 25

A bird does not sing because it has an answer.
It sings because it has a song.
—CHINESE PROVERB

Why are we all so afraid of not being good enough? We are as good as we are, and that's all we can ever be. We know what we know and don't know what we don't know. We can learn new things, but the learning process is awkward. We all have to be the student before we can be the expert.

Our value is in our attitude and not in our skill. Are we willing? Are we full of love? Are we patient and forgiving? These are what matter most. Not our knowledge and not our expertise. It's our raw material, after all, that is our greatest gift.

> ***I have a loving heart,***
> ***and that makes me equal to any situation.***

January 26

Though boys throw stones at frogs in sport,
the frogs do not die in sport, but in earnest.
—Bion

If, after making a comment, someone actually feels the need to say that they are "just kidding," chances are that they aren't. Chances are that they have said something intentionally hurtful, and that the barb of it has been felt. And then they pardon themselves by saying, "I'm just kidding. You know I'm just kidding, right?" And if I'm not amused, it means that I can't take a joke, and no one wants to be *that* person.

Under the guise of amusement, their quick assault is launched and executed. It's conscious and it's cruel, and yet it slips by. It is allowed and even condoned because of the two words that follow the jab—because of the "just kidding." Let's strike them from our usage. We can have fun and be silly, but let's not make a joke out of ourselves or anyone else.

If I am really kidding, people will know it, and if I am not,
then saying "just kidding" is a sorry excuse for delivering
a stinging barb. I choose to be kind instead.

29

January 27

Prayer is a life attitude.
—WALTER A. MUELLER

Having some kind of consistent connection to divine energy is crucial if we wish to experience fulfillment and calm in our lives. This connection is both the settling force and the rocket launcher for our dreams. It is intuition and guidance and home base. Life comes easier if we make little requests throughout the day for whatever we need, such as help, a change of thought, healing for a friend, a safe ride home, or inspiration and comfort.

We are like small children in the cockpit of a plane. We insist on doing the flying, but we don't even know how to turn on the engine. We sit stubbornly with our hands on the yoke, refusing to let the pilot take over. It doesn't seem to faze us that we are stuck on the ground. We are afraid we will crash if we let the pilot take off, and think it is better, and safer, to stay where we are. But we have another option, and it's a simple one. We can move over. We can sit *beside* the pilot and learn how to fly!

I trust in something bigger than me.
I am willing to learn what I don't know.

January 28

Exercise should be regarded as tribute to the heart.
—GENE TUNNEY

As our blood begins to circulate, so does our outlook on life. We are relieved from obsessive thinking as we start to move. If stopping and becoming internally quiet won't fix what ails us, then chances are that movement will!

Our solutions are generally so much simpler than we think they are. We have to stop doing whatever is creating a problem in our lives and start doing something to shift us in the direction of correction and healing. It seems difficult because we don't want to change. We want everything to improve without our having to make any effort. But the efforts required are never as huge as we think they are. If we are stuck, we can start by getting moving. Doing so allows for a new direction to appear, for space to open, and for our next step to be revealed.

If I feel lethargic and unmotivated, I get moving.
Circulating my blood will shift my mental perspective
and give me the fresh start I need.

January 29

I am the power and authority in my life.
I release the past and claim my good.
—LOUISE HAY

When we reclaim our power from those to whom we have errone-ously handed it over, it's like unveiling the Wizard of Oz behind his curtain. We have made someone, or a group of someones, bigger than they are. We have lived in fear of them, of getting in trouble, of not being liked or approved of, or whatever it is.

But we are more powerful than we realize, and we are not meant to crawl and beg. We must learn to stand on our own feet and speak our truth. And if our truth is unpopular, well then, so be it. It's better to be unpopular than to betray our beautiful selves.

I hold my power and honor my truth.

January 30

A good digestion turneth all to health.
—GEORGE HERBERT

We need a certain amount of time to process our experiences. We need to allow for reflection and consideration. We need to make sense of things and to decide how we will integrate new happenings and information into our already full lives. What spin will we put on the adventure, the meeting, the person, the day? Will we learn lessons, cop resentments, be self-critical and blaming, be resistant, or be grateful?

Somehow or other, we have to settle what's happened before we can move on. We have to take the time to make our peace.

I allow for the time I need to absorb and integrate the experiences of my life, and do not rush frantically from one thing to the next.

January 31

Be there for others, but never leave yourself behind.
—DODINSKY

The people we love don't always make the best choices for their own health, or ours. To watch the path of self-destruction run its course like a wildfire in someone we love is excruciating and painful. We want to fix them, to redirect them, to make them *see!* But they don't see, and maybe they can't.

It's a hard thing to realize that the best we can do when others are in reckless resentment and self-abuse mode is to take care of ourselves. It always feels a little bit as if we should fall apart with them. But that's not the answer—not for them, or us, or anyone. It's live and let live that's required, with our hearts open and our self-care boundaries intact.

I take care of myself first and foremost
because that's my main job. I am loving toward others,
but do not throw myself under their train
out of a sense of impetuous co-dependence.

February 1

How people treat you is their karma; how you react is yours.
—Wayne Dyer

It's hard not to get defensive when we are verbally attacked, especially when we don't see it coming. We feel sideswiped and knocked off-kilter. It's hard not to react with vigor, and maybe sometimes that's exactly what we *should* do, but usually such a reaction only serves to escalate the situation.

It's better, perhaps, to register our internal alarm and remain calm if we can—to say nothing and do nothing until we have had a chance to understand what is really being said. Sometimes, lots of times, an attack has nothing to do with us at all, and it's simply someone lashing out recklessly because of their own consuming fear.

***When I feel attacked in life, I have the patience to cool down
and consider the real reality before I respond.***

February 2

Put your heart, mind, intellect, and soul even to your smallest acts.
This is the secret of success.
—Swami Sivananda

If we think of work as a burden, and time off as our only pleasure, that puts an unreasonable expectation on our time off. In order to pay the bills, most of us have to work a fair chunk of our lives, so why not make it enjoyable somehow? And if we cannot possibly make it enjoyable, perhaps we should consider another job.

Resentment is the death of our joy, as is hostility for our co-workers, hatred for our boss, dislike of the hours and our commute, and all of our complaints in general. It all is what it is. If we approach our work and our lives with an open heart and a certain amount of love, we are bound to find some kind of pleasure. Little joys await us everywhere, but we have to be awake and aware to see them. Our mind's eye matters. Work is only work if that's the way we look at it.

I choose to accept my work as it is and enjoy it in unexpected ways.
I am grateful for the opportunity to be of service.

February 3

We are too busy mopping the floor to turn off the faucet.
—AUTHOR UNKNOWN

Who do we think we are? And why do we imagine that what we do is so important, so crucial, and so worth our angst and stress and fury and discombobulation? Why are we so uptight? Why can't we relax and enjoy the ride? We are sure that we won't get what we want, or deserve, or hope for, and that we will lose everything that matters to us. But why are we so negative? Hasn't life been good to us in the past?

Why don't we trust in the best possible outcome, no matter what? Blessings often grow from the muck. We survive, and yet we don't trust our survival. We feel happy, and then we wait for the other shoe to drop. Why are we so suspicious? Let's take what comes and be grateful for it, whatever it may be. Life can be that simple if we let it.

I trust the process of life and stop believing that just because I can't see something doesn't mean it's out to get me.

February 4

Kindness is in our power, even when fondness is not.
—SAMUEL JOHNSON

We can have a profoundly positive effect on people without being aware of it. And we can have a profoundly negative effect in the same way. We never know exactly what the people we face are dealing with in their lives—what challenges and victories and fears, what hurts and aches and susceptibilities. Something we say or do can change someone's life and point them toward the light, or send them plummeting into darkness.

We can't possibly know everything about people we are just meeting, or those we interact with in a limited context, so it's probably our best bet to be kind and compassionate, no matter what. Being righteous, we sometimes feel entitled to straighten someone out, to snap them into reality (*our* reality), or to call them out for wrongful acts, but maybe it's not our place to do this. Maybe it's rarely, if ever, our place to do this.

I feel better about myself when I am kind.

February 5

Rivers know this: there is no hurry. We shall get there some day.
—A. A. MILNE

I have turned time into an enemy. I am consumed by the feeling that there is not enough of it, not enough for what I *have* to do and what I *want* to do and for the achievement of all my dreams. I have created a fantasy of lack. I want abundance in my life but actively demonstrate scarcity. But I can change my perspective. I can remember that whatever *is* is surely enough. And that I have time for everything if I will only stop dictating the terms of my life that are not mine to dictate.

Let me do what is before me with good nature and care. Let me stop when I am tired or hungry or out of steam. I needn't insist on squashing my life into time-pressured compartments. I am strangling my hours with demands and wonder why I feel pinched.

***I stop trying to compress things into certain shapes
to fit my tight schedule.***

February 6

There is a wisdom in the body that is older and more reliable
than clocks and calendars.
—JOHN HAROLD JOHNSON

When the body needs to rest, it will insist upon it. I am learning that. It stops cooperating and gives out. Sometimes I can push it on, and push it on a bit more, but when it's absolutely had enough, it demands its recovery time. I think I can force my body this way, with willpower and medicines and magical thinking, with caffeine and energy drinks, but there is innate body wisdom over which I have no power in the end. I have to learn to listen to the whispers of my body as well as its shouts. It has things to tell me and important information to share.

I pay attention to my body and the lessons it has to teach me.

February 7

When you realize how perfect everything is
you will tilt your head back and laugh at the sky.
—Buddha

We feel the rumblings of imminent change coming like a distant thunderstorm. We feel this deep inside and try to pretend that we do not. It flashes lightning and growls far away. We know there will be wind and rain and cracks of fire. Thunder will rattle the earth. And on some level, perhaps, we look forward to the storm, but another part of us wants to pretend that the sun will stay and the coming clouds will move off in another direction.

But when change is imminent, it's imminent. We can delay it, but we cannot hold it off forever. We know inside what we need to do, but we are not ready to do it yet. We resist, and then resist some more. We fail to remember the way air feels after a thunderstorm. Everything heavy and oppressive has been blown away, and the world is fresh and crisp and invigorating.

I hear the call for change within me,
and I am willing to honor the call.

February 8

Fame is a fickle food
Upon a shifting plate.
—EMILY DICKINSON

Fame is as fleeting and illusory as the mist. So what is it about the *idea* of being famous that appeals to us ... *if* it appeals to us? Maybe we think that if we're famous, we can somehow cheat death and live on and on in posterity. Or perhaps we want to make an impact on the world to prove our importance in it, and our worth.

Perhaps we think that if we were famous we would be properly appreciated and acknowledged. We would have *fans*! But we would likely also be a target of hatred, and jealousy, and righteous judgment. Living famous, I imagine, is no different than living without fame. It's all living in the end. And the truth is that whatever we have "always wanted to be," the likelihood is that we already are. It's not out there in the future somewhere. We are writers if we write. We are dancers if we dance. We are comedians if we make people laugh. It can be that simple. We have nothing to prove in the end. We have only to be.

I drop all of the conditions I place on my self-worth.
I am okay just the way I am.

February 9

There is nothing but peace ... deep, calm, undisturbed.
—ERNEST HOLMES

We all have times in life when we are fully engaged. We are not lost in thought. We simply *are*. We are one with the moment and all that is. We are present. Maybe it's a creative project or singing our favorite song. Maybe it's an athletic endeavor or a quiet car ride through beautiful country. This sense of wholeness is available to us far more than we experience it. In fact, it's always available. It's right here and right now. It's in the simple awareness of what *is*.

> *I focus my attention on the present moment*
> *and experience well-being right where I am.*

February 10

Pain is the touchstone of all spiritual growth.
—BILL WILSON

I have learned from my pain. More than joy, the pain I have experienced has been the thing that has guided me on my way. Through pain, I have ended up discovering improved health, and I am able to share that experience with others. I am able to help them to ease *their* pain, and what a blessing there is in this!

I study pain, and it teaches me. It is the best teacher I know. I try things to feel better. I stretch and strengthen. I get quiet. I laugh. I cry. And make plenty of mistakes. Some things work and some do not. It is a constant journey of progress and refinement. But my experience has taught me that we *can* get better if we are willing to work at it, and change our habits, and keep our hearts open to hope. I am convinced that our pain comes not to punish us, as we might believe, but to teach us and guide us, and to point us toward the better way.

Pain has been my greatest teacher.
It has led me to where I am, and I am grateful to be here.

February 11

The question is not what you look at, but what you see.
—HENRY DAVID THOREAU

If what we are doing drags us down and makes us tired, I think that's a pretty good indicator that our creative imagination is not engaged. We may be going through the motions, but there's something lacking. Maybe we can come at it from a new angle. Maybe we can establish an internal state of play and bring some fun to the activity.

The worst possible thing is to think of how tired and bored we are, and how we wish we were elsewhere. Such thoughts make the experience utterly excruciating and slow time down to creeping. We have to remember the option we have. At any time, we can make the decision to pick up what's dragging. We can change our mind, and find the interest in what's in front of us. Creativity in life is not only possible, but excellent practice. It enables us to find a way to be happy no matter where we are or what we are doing.

If I'm bored with what I'm doing,
I come at it from a fresh angle.

February 12

It is like clouds rising in the sky: suddenly there,
gone without a trace. And it is like drawing a pattern on water:
it is neither born nor passes away. This is cosmic peace.
—MA-TSU

Some days my energy is buzzing with lively happiness and all possibilities, and some days it is flat and everything seems to require an extreme effort. I make the mistake of thinking that the high energy can be recalled at will, but it cannot. So I need to enjoy it while it lasts, knowing that it will change. And truthfully, I can find a way to enjoy the low energy, too. It's different, but not without its own kind of appeal.

Everything is cyclical, and rhythmic. Everything. And I have to learn to ride the cycles and be in touch with the natural order of things—the rising and setting sun, the moon, energy, hunger, internal peace and restlessness, eagerness, and exhaustion. It's all part of it, and each has its place. Whether I am bursting with new ideas or listless and dull, I am nonetheless growing. Life is like the rising and falling tides. Over and over, life rises, and falls.

I observe and appreciate the cycles of my life.
I am a part of the natural order of things.

February 13

I have humility enough to confess my errors.
—Mahatma Gandhi

I used to keep secrets. I held on to stories from my past and facts about myself with great guardedness and fear. It was a security job I took seriously, because I was sure if people only knew the things I had done and thought, they would lose all respect for me. I carried shame around like a bag of rocks.

And then, by suggestion, and through courage, I shared everything about me—my whole life story—with someone I could trust. And I discovered that I was not so bad after all, not so different from others, and that everything in my past was entirely forgivable. It even turned out that in some way, my errors and mistaken judgments actually made me beautiful—imperfect and vulnerable and human ... and beautiful. It was a relief to let go of my secrets. I realize today that things are only a big deal if I refuse to share them.

***It's okay to make mistakes, and I don't have to pretend
to be perfect. Sharing my secrets brings me closer to others
and lightens my load.***

February 14

Nobody has ever measured, not even poets, how much the heart can hold.
—ZELDA FITZGERALD

This is the day to express our gratitude and affection with poetic style, with flowers and love notes, fancy dinners, and romantic gifts. It is a day to fully appreciate all of the best qualities in the one we love. It's easy and fun for those of us with obvious valentines to fuss over, and even for those who are playing at the edge of romance. But I would challenge the single among us, who often mope and feel depressed on this day, to be a valentine to the self.

Let's buy a bouquet to please our own personal sense of the romantic! Or treat ourselves to a bubble bath and a beautiful meal. Whether we are in a relationship or not, we have to learn how to be loving with ourselves. That's our primary relationship and the one from which all others grow. We must know that we are lovable. The journey to fulfillment begins with us, right where we stand, and exactly with who we are.

I celebrate courtesy and romance today
and sing the praises of the one I love. And if it's not
some intimate other, let it begin with the appreciation of me!

February 15

Feelings are much like waves. We can't stop them from coming,
but we can choose which ones to surf.
—JONATAN MARTENSSON

Joy is fragile and easily squashed. How often do we encounter someone who seems unusually joyful and make a squashing kind of comment to them? "What are *you* so bubbly about? What's with the good mood?" We are almost accusatory. We watch their joy deflate like a popped balloon. And people make the same kind of remarks to us when *we* are feeling exceptionally good. We seem to silently agree that nobody should be allowed to be *too* happy. There's a sense of "not fair" when others are thriving and we are not.

We *could* choose to rejoice in their good humor instead, and let it wash all over us and lift our *own* mood by association. Either way, let's think before we speak. Let's celebrate the happiness of others, and if we cannot celebrate it, let's at least make the decision not to crush it with sarcasm or some other kind of clever quip. Joy is precious. Let's honor it properly and give it encouragement and permission to live.

I choose not to participate in squashing joy in myself or others.

February 16

One's life is not as fixed as one believes.
—Elizabeth Aston

I find it fascinating in life the way we head off enthusiastically in one direction, pretty clear about our goal and intention and quite sure of ourselves, and then we encounter a detour. We have to make an unexpected right turn. And that leads us down a hill and around a corner and through a town and unfamiliar neighborhoods. And then we have to turn again, and again.

And sometimes, after a detour, we return to our original course, but it is somehow changed by what we have been through. We see it differently. And sometimes the detour itself *becomes* the new path. We thought we were headed one way, but we were mistaken.

What never seems to fail, however, is that we end up exactly where we are supposed to be. We arrive as if by accident. We travel countless unanticipated curves in the road. We head off to L.A. and end up in Jackson. But we realize, when we get there, that Jackson was actually the place we were headed all along … whether we knew it or not.

I think I know where I'm going,
but I never really know for sure until I get there.

February 17

When there is anger, there is always pain underneath.
—ECKHART TOLLE

So much of anger is rooted in fear. When we lash out at others, it is usually our way of reacting to what we perceive as a frightening breach of personal security. For example, in traffic, if someone cuts us off unexpectedly and we have to slam on the brakes, our anger is mostly about the fact that our heart is racing and we thought for a second that we were going to wreck the car. But instead of admitting, "That scared me!" we say, "That driver is a jerk!" We curse the person and feel justified in our hatred and fury. But it's really misplaced fear, and nothing more than that.

We can acknowledge this in ourselves and others. Instead of going off on some tangent of fury and vengeance, we can stop and ask ourselves, "What am I afraid of?" The naked truth of the question itself largely diffuses the rage. And we can consider the same question for others. We can extend a little understanding instead of matching fear for fear.

I extend compassion wherever I encounter anger. I understand that anger is usually only fear and pain that are improperly expressed.

February 18

All happiness depends on a leisurely breakfast.
—JOHN GUNTHER

The preparation of good food requires love as a primary ingredient. Meals made with haste and hostility leave the palate in despair. The difference can be tasted and digested if we are paying attention. We consume the energy that comes from the heart of the cook.

So many of us cannot be bothered to eat well or to take the time to sit down and chew. We eat on the run and out of store-bought packages, fast food for fast living. And then we wonder why we feel such a lack of satisfaction. Our stomachs bloat and ache.

Let's take more care in the way we eat. Let's take more time. Let's savor the textures and colors of vegetables, the scents of herbs and spices, the heat of the oven, and the fire of the grill. The way we fill our plate matters. The way we eat matters. Let's prepare our nourishment with love and appreciation, and be truly grateful when we sit down to eat.

The energy in what I eat sustains me, and I honor that fact by preparing my meals with gratitude, mindfulness, and a loving heart.

February 19

Never let the fear of striking out keep you from playing the game.
—BABE RUTH

When I am attempting something unfamiliar and hoping for a specific positive outcome, it's hard to begin. I have a fear that I might make a mistake and do something that will blow my chance at success forever and ever. But the truth is that a beginning is just a beginning. It's not meant to be a home run or to strike me out of the game for all time. It's just a chance at bat. Maybe I get a base hit, or even a foul ball. Or maybe I walk. But I get another turn, and another, as long as I keep on playing.

But I'm not even in the game if I don't step up to the plate. I won't strike out, but I won't feel what it's like to hit the ball either. And it's satisfying to make contact with it, to feel the crack and watch the ball go down the line, or straight out to left field, or wherever it goes—far more satisfying than watching from the stands and being too afraid to play at all.

I take my chances and give life my best shot.
Even if I miss or strike out, it's worth swinging at the ball.
I could get a base hit and move forward in the game.

February 20

I have no desire to foresee you, only to discover you.
You can't disappoint me.
—Mary Haskell

Conditional love is a brutal business. It is love under siege, love that can be removed at any time for any reason. It's impossible to meet all of the potential conditions. They are always changing, so we must remain ever on guard. It's stressful and exhausting. We are loved for our behavior and our achievements, insofar as they line up in accordance with someone else's idea of who we should be and how we should be. We are not loved for who we are.

The healing process has to begin at the level of our beliefs. We have to learn to believe that we are lovable even when we mess up, even when we do foolish things and make bad decisions. If we can't direct a little kindness selfward and give *ourselves* a break, who will? How can we ever believe that others might love us unconditionally if we cannot feel that way about ourselves?

Unconditional love starts with the way I feel about myself.

February 21

Patience, patience, patience, is what the sea teaches. Patience and faith.
—ANNE MORROW LINDBERGH

The shifting tides of internal energy fascinate me. In the course of a single day, I feel stagnant, amplified, sleepy, invigorated, hot, cold, fearful, hopeful, alert, relaxed—you name it. I feel the whole realm of tides. I feel low tide, high tide, moon tide, and brackish. I feel whitecaps and windlessness. It's the natural inclination of movement in the universe to fill what's empty, and empty what's full. When I am drained, something comes along and trickles inspiration into me. I feel the energy shift, and my sense of vitality is restored. I ride on it like a kite in the breeze. And then, at some point or other—it always happens—I crash to the ground in a tangle of string.

What's reassuring is that we are never stuck in one energetic place. Life gives us the whole range of energies. Sometimes we are up, sometimes down, sometimes shaken, and sometimes rattled by joy. But what is always and for sure is that we cycle through the hours, and that we *do* fill up, and then empty, like the tide.

I appreciate the constantly moving tides of energy within me.

February 22

The North Wind boasted of great strength.
The Sun argued that there was power in gentleness.
—AESOP

The old adage "No pain, no gain" does not always apply. For instance, during a massage, if I experience pain, my body becomes defensive. It locks up to protect itself, tensing and tightening in alarm. I cannot be *forced* to relax. And I don't believe that exercise is supposed to be painful either. Exercises can actually feel good *while* they are being performed. The muscles fatigue, but they don't "hurt" per se, and the body enjoys the challenge and the range of motion.

I am reminded of the story where the sun and the wind compete with each other to see who can get a man to take off his coat. The message of the story is apt, it seems to me. If the forceful way we have of approaching things and people is not eliciting the hoped-for positive result, perhaps we might try a bit of sunshine instead.

I experience more success in all areas of my life when I come at things with gentle encouragement and love instead of brute force.

February 23

Progress lies not in embracing what is,
but in advancing toward what will be.
—KAHLIL GIBRAN

Little bits of effort every day in the right direction become big life changes over time. We get stronger and wiser and kinder one day at a time. We change our habits. We change our thinking. We change our behavior. Like quarters collected in a jar, our daily efforts add up.

So let's be sure we're moving in the direction in which we want to go—toward the light, and not away from it. Let's be sure that our small daily actions carry us forward in the direction of our dreams.

Little choices every day have big consequences over time,
so I make sure to choose carefully.

February 24

Your body is built for walking.
—GARY YANKER

The way we walk says more about us than we realize. It gives away our secrets. It shows the world whether we have insecurities or anger issues, if we have been beaten down by life, if we like who we are and feel good, or if we are not at all sure about anything.

Let's carry ourselves with the grace and nobility that we deserve. Let's stop shuffling around as if we are being persecuted and don't think much of ourselves. Even if we *have* been persecuted, let's rise above it in our carriage and our stride. Walking as if we are confident will make us *feel* confident.

We needn't gimp and hitch and get there however we get there. The way we move affects our state of being, so let's walk with good posture and good rhythm—because we *are* noble, and walking is one of the important ways that we honor our beautiful selves.

I walk with my chest up,
my head lifted, and a heart full of grace.

February 25

Let your love be like the misty rains, coming softly, but flooding the river.
—MALAGASY PROVERB

Genuine sadness is brimming with love. It is backed by compassion, not fear. There is tenderness and aching for what *is*, and for the way people suffer, and the way *we* suffer.

Sadness is free from self-pity and judgment and a desire to control. It is just sad—a heart wide open and a soul full of tears. Love can be so big sometimes that it wants to burst us, and for me, sadness falls into that category of love.

When we are sad, let's feel for the softness behind our sorrow, and experience the great love that is actually bubbling up from deep inside of us, even as our hearts hurt, sobs rattle our ribs, and tears stream down our faces.

> *I have a capacity for great love and great sadness,*
> *and they both come from the same place inside of me.*

February 26

Live and let live.
—AUTHOR UNKNOWN

We can be happy and okay even if the people around us are miserable. Our well-being does not depend on anyone else being any particular way. It feels wrong, or selfish, to be happy when our child, or our spouse, or our parent, is suffering. We impose suffering on ourselves so that we can suffer alongside them. But it's dysfunctional to believe that we can only be happy when everyone we care about is doing okay. That doesn't happen often. Someone is always having a bad day.

And we can let them. We make ourselves crazy when we insist that they be other than they are so that *we* can feel better. But what will truly make us feel better is to let them be. They'll work it out, or they won't. We get twisted up by forgetting that everybody has choices to make, and that giving them the freedom to make them is the most loving thing we can do, even if their decisions do not please us. If they ask our opinion, we owe them our honesty, but we do not need to spew our unsolicited judgments all over their lives.

I can be happy and whole
whether the people I love are feeling that way or not.

February 27

If you come at just any time, I shall never know
at what hour my heart is to be ready to greet you.
—ANTOINE DE SAINT-EXUPÉRY

Surprise visits and surprise parties are overrated in my opinion. There is something startling about them, and jarring almost. My body goes straight to fight-or-flight mode. I am tense and suddenly edgy, struck like a deer in the headlights. I haven't had the time or opportunity to prepare my heart.

Anticipation, on the other hand, is a wonderful thing. To know that there is going to be a party in our honor, and that people we love will be there, is spirit-food for weeks leading up to the event. Surprise in the details is one thing—unexpected guests from afar, live music, or the specific nature of the decorations, the flowers, the venue, etc.—but to drop the whole thing on us unsuspectingly is shocking, actually, and not always as much fun as it might initially seem.

I take pleasure in the anticipation of events.

February 28

Look at a day when you are supremely satisfied at the end.
It's not a day when you lounge around doing nothing;
it's when you've had everything to do, and you've done it.
—MARGARET THATCHER

There is a difference between the relaxation we feel lounging around all day and the relaxation we feel from being productive after hours of hard work. Though both have their place, I prefer the latter. It is satisfying to the core and guilt-free. Hard work is its own reward, as the saying goes. Feeling useful, experiencing ourselves making a difference—in the garden, with people, progressing along a path of achievement—these things enrich us. Hard work builds confidence and character. It exhausts us in the purest of ways. There's nothing like the end-of-day feeling after giving our all to life. It is a feeling of being sweetly drained and ready for the renewal of a good meal and a night of sleep. It is purpose fulfilled and energy efficiently burned. It's worth every ounce of effort and then some.

When I give everything to the day,
I feel profound satisfaction when the sun goes down.

February 29

The cave you fear to enter holds the treasure you seek.
—JOSEPH CAMPBELL

Some people avoid the personal at all costs. They converse about history and politics and public information. Their passions circulate around social issues and disturbing things they have read about in books or the newspaper. These people seem to lack an instinct for intimacy. They are always on guard, and highly competent in the art of distraction.

Looking for love from these people is frustrating at best. It's better, perhaps, to cease expecting anything from them, to join them in the realm of their carefully chosen topics, and to have compassion for their limited ability to access the contents of their soul. These people love us simply by showing up and making conversation. For now, and maybe forever, it's the best they can do.

I accept people's differing levels of conversational comfort and understand that the personal is too personal for some.

March 1

I know what I have given you. I do not know what you have received.
—Dr. SunWolf

Giving to others is healthy and satisfying, but giving indiscriminately, not so much. There must be some kind of exchange and some kind of appreciation. To pour our love into an empty vessel is reckless. We deplete ourselves if we give too much away. And in that case, we are easily taken advantage of and become like shark bait, attracting abusers to us with our puppy-like willingness.

Sometimes the most loving thing we can do is to say no. We are not meant be martyrs and draw suffering to us. We are meant to recognize what and who is before us, and be respectful, certainly, and polite, but not blind. It is our responsibility to protect ourselves from those who would rob us of what we are willing to freely give.

I treat everyone with courtesy, but give the gifts of my spirit with care. I do not wear out my brightness on those who want to dull me down.

March 2

Everything will be all right in the end,
and if it's not all right, then it's not yet the end.
—INDIAN SAYING

Why do we always go to the worst possible scenario as the likely outcome? We make assumptions based on fear, negativity, and a tremendous lack of trust—in ourselves, in our bodies, and in the rolling currents of life. We are sure this terrible thing is going to happen, or that terrible thing.

But as far as I know, none of us has ever had to deal with anything that simply could not be handled. Whatever it is, we end up handling it, with help if we need it, and one little bit at a time, we evolve through the process. We face tough situations, and yet we endure, and even with a certain amount of humor and grace. In general, things usually turn out better than we think they will. So let's imagine that it will be okay, whatever *it* is, and that it might not be a disaster and the worst possible thing after all.

> **Whatever happens, or might happen,**
> **I trust that it will ultimately be okay.**

March 3

We cannot get grace from gadgets.
—J. B. PRIESTLY

Perhaps prosperity is more of an internal state than an external one. We can have all the money we need and everything material we could possibly want, and still feel deprived. Or we can live hand to mouth and feel abundantly blessed. Riches come in the form of good health, appreciation of small pleasures, the experience of love, giving and receiving kindness, creativity, humor, friendship, and meaningful communication, as well as whopping numbers in our stock portfolios and mansions and memberships at private clubs.

Fretting over money takes a lot of time and effort. If we only had *more*, we think, we would be happier. But happy is an inside job. Happy is a choice. Happy does not come from having *more* of anything in particular. It is simply the result of being grateful.

***Insofar as I am able to experience pleasure in being alive,
I am prosperous.***

March 4

We either make ourselves miserable, or happy and strong.
The amount of work is the same.
—Francesca Reigler

What energy do we bring to the activities of our days? Do we rush through them? Are we visibly annoyed? Tired and dragging? Do we have enthusiasm? Do we smile? Do we scowl? Are we put-upon? Inflexible? Quick to anger? Do we welcome the morning and enjoy whatever happens? Or do we manufacture problems in our minds and project disasters all over our future and have a bad time? Do we experience life as hard? Are we willing to try new things? Do we complain about the status quo? Are we friendly? Cheerful? How do we approach our work, our home, our hours of daylight? Are we spending our minutes wisely? They are non-refundable.

Our attitude matters. Let's choose it with care.

I engage my energy with good intention and an open heart.
I choose to have a pleasant day, no matter what happens.

March 5

We worry away our lives.
—Lewis Thomas

I accept that some individuals like me and wish me well and that others do not. I take it further and imagine that people have strong opinions about who I am and the way I do things. I build whole cases and conditions around a look they give me. I think they're mad at something that I said or didn't say, that I did or didn't do. I fret over imaginary issues and come up with strategies to make things right.

And then something simple happens between us—a pleasant exchange of words, a smile, a demonstration of kindness—and I realize that my projections have all been wrong. There is no issue except for the one I've created in my mind. I want to remember this the next time I set off running with thoughts that someone is displeased with me. I want to allow instead for the very real possibility that they are overwhelmed with their own life and not actually thinking about me at all.

> *I resist the temptation to make assumptions*
> *about what other people think.*

March 6

Enough is as good as a feast.
—ENGLISH PROVERB

We want things to be "just right," and let's face it, they are best that way. A hot day is made pleasant by a breeze and rustling leaves. No breeze at all makes the heat oppressive, and too much of a breeze blows things all over us and whips at our skin. Just so, too much change in our lives at one time is unsettling, but not enough change feels stagnant. We want just the right amount of challenge and evolution and just the right amount of growth. Just right is just right.

Balance is about finding comfort between the extremes. That is where satisfaction awaits us—not in excess and melodrama, not in doing everything to the max and pushing all limits, but somewhere centered and grounded and comfortable, somewhere in between. We find our satisfaction in the place in the middle, the place that is just right ... for us.

> *I seek balance in my life and avoid the lopsided*
> *attraction of excessive extremes.*

March 7

Well-timed silence hath more eloquence than speech.
—MARTIN FARQUHAR TUPPER

We must allow people their dignity. If we observe someone speaking in error or doing something that we feel could use correction, we can take the time and consideration to choose our moment and our method to make a suggestion. We needn't call out everything we see. We needn't make people wrong. We can be subtle. We can be kind. We can consider the most loving approach to others and ask ourselves if what we have to say really needs to be said.

We can spare people embarrassment by pausing briefly to think before we speak, and consider the consequences before we blurt out our opinion. Our opinion is not as important as allowing another human being their dignity and self-respect.

I don't have to express everything I think.
I consider thoughtfully before I open my mouth.

March 8

Everything has beauty, but not everyone sees it.
—Confucius

There's something beautiful in everyone. We have to be attentive and be willing to look, but it's there. I guarantee it. There are the things that are obviously beautiful in others, and then there are the things that not everyone can see—a particular turn of the cheek, robust hips, a graceful way of moving, trembling speech, wisps of hair at the temple: the subtleties of being.

Multitudes of people are blocked from seeing their own beauty as well as the beauty in others. Let's not be among them. Let's look for treasures in people instead of flaws, for gifts and talents instead of liabilities. And if we see the beauty in others, and make a habit of seeing it, then perhaps we can truly learn to experience it in ourselves.

Beauty is a way of seeing.
I see beauty everywhere I look.

March 9

Men's natures are alike; it is their habits that separate them.
—CONFUCIUS

We get to a point in life where we are tired of feeling lousy all the time, so we make changes in our habits and our lifestyle. And then, we start to feel better. Life looks up. We forget how it used to be. Over time, we begin to take our newfound health for granted, and slowly, slowly, we slip back into our old ways. We stop doing the things that make us feel good.

I'm convinced that health is largely the result of daily maintenance. If we don't bother to take care of ourselves, on any front, we will feel the difference. It's easy to use stress and difficulties as excuses to let our good habits slide, and yet that is when we need them the most! To feel our best in any and all situations, we need to maintain our good habits no matter what, every day, for a lifetime.

I take care of myself so I can enjoy my life.

March 10

The problem in defense is how far you can go without destroying
from within what you are trying to defend from without.
—Dwight D. Eisenhower

Learning to pick our battles is an important life skill. Sometimes we take a righteous stand against something that we don't actually have the power to change, and end up paying a higher penalty than we anticipated. No matter how right we may be, we have to calculate the potential losses that will result from taking up arms. We have to realistically determine if it's worth it to fight.

We live in a sloppy world. Lack of integrity abounds, as does lack of reason and common sense. We are all limited, to a certain extent, and imposed upon by rules and regulations that we don't necessarily agree with. But most of them are enforceable nonetheless, and if we want to participate, we have to find a way to get along. Being right may not always be as important as being at peace. We have to pick our battles with care, and be honest about the real cost of things.

> *I make sure I'm willing to pay the price*
> *of contention before I engage.*

March 11

Love is absolute loyalty.
—SYLVESTER STALLONE

I feel a powerful loyalty to the people I care about. I feel protective of them. I have an interest in who they are and what they're up to. I care about what happens to them, how they feel, and what makes them happy ... and sad. From a certain angle, caring as much as I do might be considered a liability. But I choose it. I choose caring over not caring. Caring connects me to life, and to people, and work. Caring gives these things meaning beyond the ordinary.

I might be able to make more money if I were less loyal, and I might have a more raging sort of personal freedom. But I might also feel less connected to the world I live in, and probably also feel less joy in my heart. It makes me happy to love people. It makes me happy all the way through. So I'll keep on loving them, and keep on caring, and keep on feeling grateful every day that I am a part of something so much bigger than myself.

I get to know the people I encounter regularly and allow myself to care about them, without apology and with my full heart.

March 12

We can only be said to be alive in those moments
when our hearts are conscious of our treasures.
—THORNTON WILDER

It's an incredible thing to survive an accident that could have been fatal if things had played out only slightly differently. There's a moment of clear recognition that life is fragile, terribly fragile, and precious, and that we take it for granted far too easily.

Accidents are accidents for a reason. We don't anticipate them, and they have the ability to rock our world. They come as a reminder—that we are here by grace, ultimately, and grace alone. Given that truth, it seems to me that gratitude is our best operating system. Gratitude that we are here! That we taste and smell and feel and dream! That we are able to hope ... and love! That we wake up and have the ability to enjoy yet another beautiful day! There are countless many who are not so lucky.

I do not take my breath and beating heart for granted.
I am grateful to be alive.

March 13

The sea does not reward those who are too anxious, too greedy,
or too impatient... One should lie empty, open, choiceless as a beach—
waiting for a gift from the sea.
—ANNE MORROW LINDBERGH

On the back of certain dump trucks are the words "DO NOT PUSH." The letters are bold, and the message clear. I take it to heart every time I see it, and am reminded that pushing and forcing and insisting usually get me no place but stuck.

Understanding the natural rhythm and flow of life situations, and relationships, and moods, is crucial to finding peace and relaxation. It makes us forgiving and tolerant and able to patiently wait for a shift in the direction of things. Energy is constantly on the move, so we have to learn to ride the currents much like we learn to body-surf the waves.

"Do not push" is excellent advice. The longer I live, the more it seems to me that real power lies in our ability to surrender to what is—to cease fighting, to let go and let be. And then, when all is settled, it's time to let go some more.

I stop pushing against everything I come up against
and make a decision to go with the flow.

March 14

The best things in life must come by effort from within.
—FRED CORSON

There is a point at which our doing for others actually disables them. This fact is important to recognize, particularly for parents, and perhaps even more so for mothers than for fathers. Years of taking care of our children's needs can form a caretaking habit. But we have to outgrow it at some point, or we become agents of stunting growth. We have to let them—children, lovers, friends, parents, whoever—take responsibility for their own journey, their own momentum, and their own daily care.

By feeling compelled to smooth over all of the rough edges for the people we love, and make it all okay for them no matter what, and to "do" for them, and fuss and bother over them constantly, we kill their autonomy. We can love—yes! We can love with our whole selves, but real love doesn't mean "doing for." Real love is about trusting others to know what they need and giving them the reins and the freedom to establish their own ground.

> *I stop taking care of others who are more than*
> *capable of taking care of themselves.*

March 15

I will not let anyone walk through my mind with their dirty feet.
—Mahatma Gandhi

We live in a culture of spin doctors. People are constantly telling us that this, that, or the other thing is good for us, will benefit us, will be the best possible thing for us, when the reality is that our biting on their bait won't actually benefit us at all. It will benefit them. We are told that things that are clearly unreasonable are reasonable, and that scenarios that are sketchy have no risk involved—that they're free! When they're not, actually. All this false advertising teaches us to questions our instincts.

We have a strong internal red-flag warning system for a reason. The cost is high when we ignore its signals. Let's not. Let's honor our gut, and trust that our knowing is solid and our instinct for danger is likely right on. Let's not be afraid to say no, as many times as it takes, and let's watch out for the snake-oil salesmen who abound.

I have to be my own advocate. Those who want to sell me something don't usually have my best interest at heart.

March 16

When you say or do anything to please, get, keep, influence,
or control anyone or anything, fear is the cause and pain is the result.
—BYRON KATIE

We spend so much time trying to solve potential problems. We imagine the possible scenarios and have an answer for each one. But inevitably, it is the thing that hasn't even crossed our mind that actually happens. Our strategic plans are abandoned as we face whatever has come.

Let's work on quieting our minds when they take us into future crises. Let's pull ourselves gently back to the present moment and reassure ourselves in the here and now. What's right in front of us is our responsibility—not some fantasy drama from next month, or next year.

We can't possibly know for certain about the future, so why do we try? We create a reality where there is none and make ourselves problem-solving heroes in the imaginary future. We try to guarantee our own safety. But the only *real* safety is right where we are.

> *In this moment, and in every moment,*
> *I am equal to whatever may befall me.*

March 17

You have the answer. Just get quiet enough to hear it.
—Pat Obuchowski

Nobody likes to be told what to do. Someone else dictating to us what's best, or what we need, or what we *should* do, is distasteful. The rebel in most of us rises up to rail against the imposition. We want it to be *our* idea. We want the credit and the sense of satisfaction that comes from the autonomy of choosing. And we would usually rather choose the *wrong* thing on our own than choose the right thing by force.

When dealing with people, let's eliminate the words "You should..." and replace them with "You could..." To feel fully alive, we all need to make our own choices. If we let others choose *for* us, we give away our power. If we think others know better than we do what is the right thing, we deplete our inner resources and dishonor our guides. I believe we are drawn to our lessons and that sometimes we actually *need* to make the choice that appears wrong to others so that we can have the opportunity to learn the exact lesson that is right... for us.

I gather opinions, but I decide for myself.

March 18

It's not easy to find happiness in ourselves,
and it's not possible to find it elsewhere.
—AGNES REPPLIER

It's an interesting and entertaining exercise to consider what we would do if we won the lottery and suddenly had access to unlimited funds. Would we buy things? Would we buy big things, little things? Jewelry? Gifts for others? Would we invest the money? Would we give it away? Take a trip? Do we think it would solve our problems? Would we move? Live in a different sort of house and neighborhood? Drive a different car? To my mind, these are provocative questions, and the honest answers to them teach me something about myself.

But if I'm being honest, I know that having oodles of money just changes the playing field. It doesn't end the game. Life is still life whether we are rich or poor. And nothing external, not even a winning lottery ticket, will guarantee our happiness. No matter what we have, or don't have, happiness is ultimately and forever an inside job.

> *If I can't be happy without winning the lottery,*
> *I will never be happy winning it.*

March 19

Our birthdays are feathers in the broad wing of time.
—JEAN PAUL RICHTER

Birthdays are tough for me. Much as I might want the day to be ordinary, there is always that small thing within me that has an expectation that it should be more—more than just another day. It should be special, indulgent, and exceptionally fulfilling. I have whispering thoughts inside of me of all the possible wonders that *could* happen, the fantastic surprises that just *might* be coming my way. I apply my own kind of self-inflicted birthday pressure, and that sets me up for disappointment.

If I am able to relax and open to gratitude and the love in my heart, my birthday generally ends up better than I could have planned. There are people who love me, and I always get just what I need, and delightful surprises of some kind or another to boot ... if I can drop my expectations and get out of my own way.

I trust in the perfect unfolding of each day,
even the special ones. I don't need to orchestrate my life.

March 20

When you sit, let it be.
—Ajahn Chah

I am not a fan of loose ends. And it's easy for me to overthink a problem, trying to solve it so I can tie up the end. I chew on it like a dog with a bone. But there comes a point at which I have to stop, where my fretting is actually working against me and I am further than ever from a solution by trying too hard to find one.

I have to free up the energy around the situation by turning my attention elsewhere. I have to let the problem breathe, and then return to it fresh. The answer always comes, not by my insisting upon it but more often by my absolute willingness to let it go.

I cannot get what I want by grabbing for it. I have to sit back and call it gently to me. I have to let it come of its own accord.

March 21

Conquer the angry man by love. Conquer the ill-natured man by goodness.
Conquer the miser with generosity. Conquer the liar with truth.
—THE DHAMMAPADA

It always surprises me when people are cruel. Most of the individuals I interact with are reasonable and gracious, thoughtful and fundamentally kind, more often than not. But occasionally I find myself at the receiving end of someone's emotional whip. They lash me on purpose, and it hurts.

But beyond the hurt, I have great compassion for those who are cruel. It seems sad to me that they should feel the need to be so vindictive. I lick my wounds and send out blessings, and remind myself that cruelty happens and that I can get caught in its crossfire, which is no fun. So I better keep a lookout and, whenever possible, stay out of the way.

I send out armies of compassion
to transmute cruelty when it barbs and stings.

March 22

If you want to be happy, be so.
—KOZMA PRUTKOV

Love is awake and aware, never scared, prepared,
Full of care and fairness.

Bare your heart and mind, be kind, unwind,
And take your time.

Bestow hope, avoid dope, and find a way to cope
With life the way it is.

Because it doesn't get any better than this.

I look to this day with joy!

March 23

It is much easier to become a father than to be one.
—Kent Nerburn

Here is a salute to all of the good fathers out there! Thank you for being loving and encouraging, patient and supportive. Thank you for your guidance and your groundedness, your broad shoulders, and your ability to forgive the foolishness of youth.

Let's celebrate the nobility and generosity of good fathers, with their twinkling humor and their kind hearts. And to all of those fathers who are not so kind and forgiving, and those who have abandoned their children, and abused them, and been less than generous, let's feel grateful anyway. We thank you for the gift of life.

Blessings to all of the fathers of the world! We celebrate you! We accept and appreciate you for all that you are, and all that you are not.

I am grateful for my father in spite of his shortcomings.
I have shortcomings of my own.

March 24

Boundaries need to be clear and unapologetic.
—DR. HENRY CLOUD

Personal space is about more than physical distance. It's a necessary protection against the creeping energy of meddlesome others. Their invasive questions can thrust across our boundaries before we even realize that we need to shore them up. Boundaries are necessary and respectable. We cannot hope for satisfaction in life if we recklessly disrespect them in others, or allow them to disrespect ours.

To reestablish a boundary once it has been broken, we have to send out a volley or warning to ward off the perpetrators. We have to pause a moment to repair the damage. Like a dog who growls, we have to be clear with others when they are overstepping. Inviting them to tromp all over us with their thoughts and opinions and questions is to become their toy. We lose our footing as they push at us. We need to learn to stand our ground.

> ***I understand and appreciate the importance***
> ***of personal boundaries.***

March 25

Gratitude is an opener of locked-up blessings.
—MARIANNE WILLIAMSON

The thing that has the power to transform self-pity and discontent into something more palatable is gratitude. If we are feeling particularly petulant, we may whine that we have nothing at all to be grateful for. But that, of course, is ridiculous and untrue.

I'm grateful for sunshine and nighttime and deep sleep. I'm grateful that I can see and hear, that I can touch and taste. I'm grateful for friendship and laughter, for air conditioners when it's hot, and heat when it's cold. I'm grateful for flowers and thunderstorms and fruit. Gratitude builds on itself. One thing leads to another and another, and before we know it, we are feeling better.

I am grateful for gratitude! And for the knowledge that if I'm feeling pouty, I don't have to stay that way. I can count my blessings and express my thanks—and in so doing, I am transformed from misery to abundance, and petulance to joy!

I accept and acknowledge my blessings
and let the energy of gratitude wash over me like rain.

March 26

To give up enthusiasm wrinkles the soul.
—SAMUEL ULLMAN

We use "tired" as an excuse for anything and everything. We are too tired to participate, to exercise, to eat well, to dress well, to communicate, to be pleasant ... What makes us so tired? Is it a cover story for being disinterested? Bored? Afraid? Perhaps it is the simple result of our lively spirit being overtaxed. We want to be playful and delight in life, and instead we feel oppressed with the weight of daily obligations and requirements and bills. Tired is heavy and burdensome. It is trudging and old.

If we feel tired a great deal, perhaps it is a message for us. Perhaps we need to reevaluate the way we spend our time, the way we exert our energy, and the way we pour our vitality out into the world. Maybe we are wasteful about it. Maybe we are not honoring our hearts. Maybe we are so duty-bound that we are missing the calling of our small joys.

If I'm always tired, I'm willing to do some soul-searching to discover what my fatigue is all about, and honestly consider the changes I need to make to restore vitality to my life.

March 27

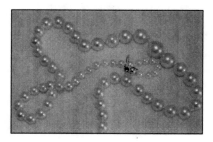

There are exactly as many special occasions in life
as we choose to celebrate.
—Robert Brault

Any day can be a great day. It doesn't matter if it's Monday or Friday, rainy or clear, empty of activity or full of errands. What makes the day good or bad is the way we approach it. If we are happy to go along and get along, then we can have one great day after another. If, on the other hand, we insist that things be a particular way, if conditions have to be perfect before we can consider the day a success, then we will likely have bad days instead of good ones, and plenty of them.

It's important to remember that we have the power to change our mind about things at any time and as often as we please. Nothing makes the day lousy but the way we sell it to ourselves: as pain and suffering or as a grand adventure. Let's make the decision to choose adventure and have one great day after another, like pearls on a string.

Whatever may or may not happen, I choose to enjoy the day.

Never lose an opportunity of seeing anything that is beautiful ...
thank God for it as a cup of blessing.
—RALPH WALDO EMERSON

Certain weeds have pretty flowers. They are wild and uncultured. They grow by the roadside and in the woods and by the edge of fields. They pop up and bloom with stickers and thorns. They remind me that beauty is not limited to the mainstream of life. It is not limited by anything. It is sometimes restless and sometimes poised, but regardless of the moment and the view, it is always fresh and authentic—true to itself. Beauty is unapologetic and innocent. It doesn't know it's beautiful. It simply is what it is, and as such, it takes our breath away.

I recognize and experience beauty in the most unlikely of places.
It surprises and delights me.

March 29

There is nothing either good or bad, but thinking makes it so.
—SHAKESPEARE

Often, we seek a big external fix when all that's actually needed is a small internal adjustment. Nine times out of ten, a shift in attitudinal approach will cure what ails us. We become frantic with our figuring and planning, and all the things that have to change immediately, and what it will all mean, and how it will work or not work…

But if we just change the angle of our perspective slightly, and restore ourselves to gratitude and faith, we may discover that nothing is broken after all, that nothing actually needs fixing. Our problem is mysteriously resolved, and all we had to do to get there was to look at things a little differently.

Before I panic and think I have to change everything in my life
to feel okay, I get quiet and become willing to change
my perspective on things just the way they are.

March 30

A sense of humor is just common sense, dancing.
—WILLIAM JAMES

We take ourselves too seriously. We fret and fuss and overthink everything. We allow ourselves to get weighed down with daily burdens and responsibilities. We count on life being difficult and make struggling a daily habit.

But maybe the whole point of life is to take ourselves and our life circumstances *less* seriously, and to find the fun in *whatever* we do. It's there. If we approach things playfully, they are enjoyable, and we laugh easily and feel relaxed. If, on the other hand, we approach them with dread, then our foreheads wrinkle, and dread is what we feel.

I am willing to take myself less seriously
and to live life with more laughter and less intensity.

March 31

Music washes away from the soul the dust of everyday life.
—BERTHOLD AUERBACH

It's important and necessary that we make time to sing at the top of our voices and to dance. We need to find a way to honor the songs that resonate within us, and to fully enjoy the rising experience of the rhythm and the beat. Without allowing for such a musical expression on some kind of a regular basis, no matter our age, it seems to me that we live our lives "in check"—properly restrained and composed, but missing out on a piece of freedom.

It's a primal thing to let go. Let's give ourselves permission. Let's crank up the tunes and get our bodies moving. It's heartening. It's joyful. And it's fun!

I sing along to my favorite songs and dance with joy
to the music that moves me.

April 1

The world we have created is a product of our thinking.
—ALBERT EINSTEIN

We are what we think about. We create a reality that is beautiful or oppressive, hostile or friendly. We create suffering and pestilence, or blessings galore. The real reality of our situation is no more complicated than the way we think about it. Do we look on the bright side? Do we expect the best? Do we believe that things will work out? Or are we victims?

With our thoughts, we create our world, every minute of every day, and we are free to change at any time and in any direction we choose. There is power in this. It is the power of creation and manifestation. Considering this, let's adjust ourselves and our expectations and judgments to improve the quality of our day, and our year, and our whole life experience.

I observe my thoughts and see how I am sabotaging myself with negativity. I am willing to change the way I think to experience more satisfaction in my life.

April 2

You can't change the world. The best you can do is learn to live with it.
—HENRY MILLER

It's true that in life "it's always something." The minute we feel that we are in the clear at last—free from pain, free from debt, secure in love, whatever it may be—here comes the next challenge and the new discomfort. There is no quick fix, no absolute security, and no point of arrival. There is always the next step and the next thing. Our back feels better and then our elbow starts acting up. The elbow heals and we step on a rusty nail. We are poisoned by food, the car breaks down, our dog gets skunked, or someone dies and we find ourselves utterly unprepared emotionally.

We have to learn how to get comfortable being off-balance. Like a tightrope walker, we have to learn to constantly shift our weight and energy and attention to keep from toppling over. Life is a tightrope. We have to learn to accommodate ourselves to the height and instability.

I can be comfortable and secure no matter what.
Life is a dynamic adventure of adaptability.

April 3

Restless thoughts ... rush upon me thronging.
—John Milton

Obsessive thinking is exhausting. It consumes our energy like wildfire. If we are lucky, we can stop it, but it's difficult to keep it stopped. Like a broken record, the mind catches again in the same spot, and gets stuck there, circling around and around. It's addictive and gnawing, a nail-biting habit—both destructive and strangely appealing at the same time. Perhaps we obsess mentally over things because the fantasy drama we create seems controllable somehow and gives us a false sense of power. It keeps us from having to face what we don't want to face.

But in the end, obsessive thinking can't save us. The only salvation is in embracing the moment, and being present and attentive. Projections of all kinds cast shadows on the screen of blessing that is right in front of us. We miss the simple and abundant grace that is already here by creating faraway fantasies. We miss the breeze and the singing of birds as we turn ourselves into imaginary heroes and take the world by storm.

> *I recognize when I am hooked by obsessive thinking,*
> *and return to the moment.*

April 4

To affect the quality of the day, that is the highest of arts.
—Henry David Thoreau

We have the ability to lift each other up. When we encounter someone who is having a bad day, who is overwrought with stress or negativity, we can spread a bit of cheer upon them. If we are quiet and grounded, if we do not take their darkness personally and get defensive, if we listen and acknowledge their hardships and are willing to share related stories from our own experience, then we can change the quality of their day.

It's about love. It's about a willingness to be loving. It comes from compassion and an open heart and the ability to see. If we pay attention, we can *see* worry and stress in others. We can *see* fear and resentment, and we can sense these things as well. And with our love, we can dispel them. We can scatter the darkness in others by spreading our own light.

When I encounter people who are full of darkness and stress,
I center myself and engage my compassion.
I watch them soften and sweeten as I shower them with love.

Right action is the key to good living.
—BILL WILSON

Everything in life is a mixed experience. In order to have good times and good feelings, we have to be willing to do the footwork. We cannot enjoy the feeling of being fit unless we are willing to exercise our bodies. We cannot enjoy being in a healthy relationship unless we are willing to communicate honestly and take responsibility for our part in conflicts. In every job and every experience, there is both joy *and* effort. Neither one exists without the other.

Culturally, we seem to believe that it's possible and desirable to live a life of leisure without contributing anything meaningful to it. And we erroneously think that such a life is worth aiming for. But nothing is given without something being taken. Life is an exchange. It's give *and* take. Taking alone is unsustainable and unsatisfying. It is only when we have planted the seeds and weeded and watered the crop that we can truly appreciate the harvest.

I do my part. In the exchange of life,
I work hard, and then I reap the benefits.

April 6

Humor is the great thing, the saving thing after all. The minute it crops up, all our hardnesses yield, all our irritations, and resentments flit away, and a sunny spirit takes their place.
—MARK TWAIN

We can nudge people into seeing that they are taking themselves too seriously, and be nudged in the same way by others. A gentle tease and a loving smile go a long way toward relaxing what is up-tight and rigid: a reminder that nothing is worth losing our sense of humor over, or our cool.

Life happens. Sometimes it's inconvenient. Sometimes it's expensive. Sometimes it's inopportune. But what are we going to do? Being grouchy changes nothing. We have to learn to roll with the punches and dive under the waves. If we fight them, they batter us. But if we work with the currents and learn to go with the flow, we are carried and sustained.

> *I move with the tides. I keep my sense of humor*
> *and allow for the mutability of life.*

April 7

Let go or be dragged.
—AMERICAN PROVERB

It's easier to become aware of the fact that I am holding tension than it is to let it go, and I'm not sure why that is. Perhaps the tension is restraining some sort of emotional outburst in me that I don't want to express or experience. So maybe it's a hiding as well as a holding, and that's what makes it harder to face. Maybe it's sadness underneath the tension, or maybe it's fear. Whatever it is, I believe that mostly it just wants to have a voice.

Why do we resist what we feel? And why do we think we shouldn't be feeling it? We force happiness upon ourselves and insist upon it, and beat ourselves up for not feeling it—as if we *should* be feeling it, every minute of every day. But sometimes happiness actually comes to us in the form of sadness or fear that is freely and unapologetically expressed. Whatever we feel is okay. So let's ease up and allow ourselves to be where we are.

I recognize tension as a cover story for unexpressed emotion and have the courage to properly acknowledge what I'm feeling in order to experience relief.

April 8

There is power, and then there is power, my dear.
—Tamara Pierce

We have levels of power within us. The most superficial one is limited in its lasting ability. It burns out in a flash of high-intensity effort. But beneath it is more power—a bit less accessible, but stronger, and with more endurance. This second level can carry us far, but eventually it, too, is spent.

At the deepest level, we are unlimited in our power. We can engage physical strength beyond our wildest dreams. It's our low gear and four-wheel drive. But we cannot use this power without focus. We cannot use it without our breath and intention and heart. It is a conscious shift into super-human power mode, the rising up of pure life force energy. Knowing that we have this kind of power available to us, and learning to access it on demand, will take us beyond the possible into the realm of the miraculous time and again. So when we feel burnt out, let's focus and breathe and call up our resources from the depths. Let's learn to engage our low gear.

I learn to use my breath and intention
in order to access my unlimited power mode.

April 9

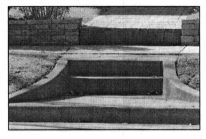

Love yourself first and everything else falls into line.
—LUCILLE BALL

We are far too readily self-deprecating. We cut ourselves down with our words and thoughts. We are so stupid, weak, clumsy, messed up, fat, out of shape, or bad at this, that, or the other thing. It's a dangerous business, and none of it is true. We may not be exactly where we want to be, but we will never get there believing in our own worthlessness.

We are beautiful beings of light and promise who have been battered by the winds of life. But we are not down for good unless we make the decision to stay down. We are in flux at all times, either improving our condition or condemning ourselves to misery. Let's choose the improvement route and feel better and better every day! Gently, we must acknowledge where we could make positive changes and then become willing to make them, and give ourselves credit for every faltering step we take, and grant ourselves forgiveness for all of our stumbles and trips.

I do not denigrate myself. I appreciate the effort I make
to do the right thing, and give myself a break
if the results aren't always perfect.

April 10

In the middle of difficulty lies opportunity.
—ALBERT EINSTEIN

I seem to cruise happily along the road of life, and then hit a patch of potholes. Something triggers me and I find myself suddenly focused on what's wrong, jarred by the bumps. I am overcome unexpectedly with darkness. Hours of smooth pavement and pleasure in the ride become marred uncomfortably with my sudden irritability.

And then, the rough road is just as suddenly behind me and it is smooth sailing yet again. It feels erratic to me. I'd like to be able to transition with more grace, or learn to somehow not lose my pleasure in the potholes at all. I don't think it *has* to be that way. I believe I can learn to laugh when I bounce. I believe it's possible to live without crashing every time I encounter a dip.

I recognize when I hit potholes in my day and don't let them sink me. I trust that the road will smooth out yet again.

April 11

We live by an invisible sun within us.
—Thomas Browne

It's okay to be who we are. It's okay to love what we love, and to laugh at the things that strike us as funny, and to cry at whatever moves us to tears. It's okay to be a little pudgy, or skinny, or muscular, or lanky. It's okay to have any and every combination of imperfect body parts. It's okay to need time alone, to want to be with people, to take naps, eat desserts, or be a vegetarian. Authentic living does not apologize for itself.

If we squash ourselves to fit some mold, or live according to specific cultural ideals or expectations, we will suffer for it. We are meant to be true to ourselves and to contribute to the world what we alone can contribute—our unique combination of life and heart and body and soul. We are love in action when we are who we are. When we are ourselves, the joy of self-expression radiates off of us like sun rays, and we light the path we travel and illuminate the people we touch.

> *I do not apologize for being who I am.*
> *I glory in self-expression.*

April 12

Actions express priorities.
—Charles A. Garfield

What are the priorities in our lives? What do we make important? What is disposable and what is absolutely non-negotiable? What's the most important thing, and who's the most important person? Do we make time for the things we love? Are *we* disposable? Do *our* needs matter less than the needs of our spouse or our children or our parents or friends? Do we *have* friends? Do we make *them* a priority?

Let's think about it. How do we measure the pieces and the portions of our lives?

I realistically examine my priorities
to see what they say about me,
and I become willing to move things around
in order to honor my truth.

Be careful how you interpret the world: It is like that.
—ERICH HELLER

Misconstrue is a good word and is applicable to more of our life experience than we can possibly realize. We misconstrue our responsibilities, and our power to control things. We misconstrue people and outcomes and motives and meanings. We manufacture a personal reality based on our thoughts and our skewed understanding of how people feel, and what we think they want and need. We get all tangled up in strings.

If we aren't sure and don't know absolutely the how and why and where and what of something that happens in life, let's call it for what it is and admit that we don't know. And if we are meant to know, we will, and if we are not, we won't. Some things become clear as they unfold, or we understand them in hindsight, and some things aren't ever going to make logical sense to us. They simply are what they are, and that's the most we will ever get.

**Knowing how easily I misconstrue situations and words,
I am willing to make room in my thinking for the fact that
I may not understand the real reality.**

April 14

If you want to find the secrets of the universe, think in terms of energy, frequency, and vibration.

—Nikola Tesla

Life is magnetic. We are drawn to certain things and people and places, and repulsed by others. I can't help but think that what we are drawn to has a meaning, a lesson, or a gift for us, and that if we discount the pull, we will miss out. I believe we are meant to explore things, sometimes shallowly and sometimes deeply, and that our exploration often takes courage that we are hard-pressed to muster. It seems easier to say that the grapes are sour before we have even spotted the vine.

But what's our point in being here anyway, in being alive? Is it about safety? Is it about maintaining the status quo? Or is it about trying things and following leads and having the faith to take a risk—and then trusting ourselves enough to know when it's time to return home?

> *I trust myself to explore the things I'm drawn to,*
> *and then to make good decisions as I follow the path.*

April 15

Sometimes I've believed as many as six impossible things before breakfast.
—Lewis Carroll

Our lessons and inspirations sometimes come from the most unlikely places. We project and pre-judge, and write things and people off without clearly understanding what value they might have for us. We live our lives in discount mode. We discount others and we discount ourselves. We are arrogant and think we know everything about everything, or else we are so ruled by fear that we become paralyzed and refuse to grow.

Let's live in the draft of an open mind on all fronts, and be patient. Let's be willing to wait and see and entertain the concept of maybe. We are impulsive. We say yes to this and no to that—without thought, without consideration, and without the element of possibility in the mix. Let's open ourselves to the idea that *anything* is possible, and that we never know what unlikely event or encounter could positively change the entire course of our lives.

I keep an open mind and do not shut down ideas out of habit.
I am willing to experience the possible in all walks of life.

April 16

Decide that you want it more than you are afraid of it.
—BILL COSBY

Fear is a lame excuse, and it's at the root of all of our excuses. We are afraid of pain, of difficulty, of failure. We are afraid of the unknown. We are that afraid we will look silly, or not be able to keep up, or that we will experience discomfort. Even when there are things that we want, things that we have wanted for a long time and have worked particularly hard to achieve, we get close to getting them and then throw in the towel. Never mind, we tell ourselves. Who are we kidding?

We retreat to what we know, and feel a certain relief, but not really. We have bailed on our hopes and played it safe. We have taken a seat and abandoned the actualizing of our vision. And as a result of our sudden inaction, the fear dissipates, but so does the excitement, and we are left flat. We have flattened ourselves. Let's acknowledge our fear but not let it squash us. Let's believe in our path, and our dreams, even if it's scary, even if we can't see far ahead, and even if we have no idea how it's all going to turn out in the end.

I feel my fear but don't let it stop me.
I trust in the calling of my dreams.

April 17

If you have integrity, nothing else matters.
If you don't have integrity, nothing else matters.
—Alan Simpson

Respect yourself. Respect others. Respect the environment. These three statements say it all and apply on every level. They seem so reasonable. But simple as they are, it's hard not to fall short one way or the other. Of course we should respect the environment, and yet we pollute it, both culturally and personally. We take the natural world for granted. And we're able to respect *some* people, but we have little tolerance and lots of judgment for most others. And when it comes to *self*-respect, we are generally reckless. We easily abuse ourselves with critical thoughts, with stress, and food, and extreme behavior.

Let's improve our level of respect for all things by raising our awareness. Let's become mindful of what we send out into the world.

I give respect and receive it in kind.

April 18

You must weed your mind as you would weed your garden.
—TERRI GUILLEMETS

Beginnings and transitions are always hard work because so much adjustment is required. We have to assimilate the new without abandoning our daily maintenance routines that keep us steady. We have to make room for the unknown and the unforeseen and be willing to be flexible. At first, it seems impossible that we could absorb anything additional into our already full lives, and yet we can, and we do. Life fills up just a little bit more.

But eventually, pruning is always required. We have to pare back and trim down. Though we may pile on more and more and more indefinitely, it's a pace we cannot keep. Eventually, with too much on every front, we burn out, and compromise the quality of our lives. Let's be smart. Let's grow at a sustainable rate. Let's live a life of exciting forward progress and reflective still motion. Let's regularly pause and clear the air, and our schedules, and our e-mails, and our minds, so that we can enjoy the journey and appreciate every detail of the ride.

I learn to pace myself in life, and know how to pare back
when my plate is overfull.

April 19

[Ego is the] fountain cry, origin, sole source of war!
—GEORGE MEREDITH

Our egos spew their grandiosity all over the world. Ego in action is a power trip. We push our weight around because we can. We do it with arrogance, to varying degrees. But the true test of evolution and grace, it seems to me, is to have the option, and even the legitimacy, to say, "I told you so," and to choose silence instead—to not insist on making others smaller so that we can feel bigger. If we are spiritually fit, we know that we are big enough already, and that there is no real percentage in squashing people down.

We don't have to be "greater than." We don't have to be mean and nasty. We don't have to be righteous. We can be forgiving. We can be right-sized. We can enjoy the reality of being comfortably human.

> *I recognize when my ego wants to take over,*
> *and I keep it in check. I smile, breathe deeply, relax,*
> *and remember that I have nothing to prove.*

April 20

Love what is.
—Byron Katie

The fact that nothing remains constant is actually a blessing if we look at it in the right way. It keeps life interesting, and we are sure to never get completely and irretrievably stuck. Our pain is acute, then dull and aching, then unnoticeable, and then it moves elsewhere. Our moods are light, dark, and our energy jazzed, mellow, dried up. We are talkative. We are quiet. We feel like dancing. We feel like sleeping. We laugh, cry, talk with enthusiasm, whisper. We are king of the world, victim, overdone, undone, fresh, weepy, and passionate. We are punchy. We are frantic and edgy. We can be all of these things in the course of a single day, and often are. Sometimes our vision is fuzzy, and sometimes we see like hawks. Our perfect moments do not come to stay, but neither does our trauma. It is exactly because each experience is fleeting that it is so incredibly beautiful.

I savor my moments.

April 21

If you make up your mind not to be happy there's no reason why you shouldn't have a fairly good time.
—EDITH WHARTON

When we stop grabbing at life, everything that we have been reaching for seems to come to us. We cannot receive by force, but only by grace. It is not for us to make up our minds about things and then expect them to play out exactly as we plan. When I sought to make a fortune, I went bankrupt. When I decided to wait a year to have children, I found myself pregnant with twins. When I was absolutely at peace with being by myself, I met my husband.

We have to come to the place where we know that we don't require anything in particular to be happy and feel fulfilled—not a certain amount of money, or some particular position at work; not the perfect relationship or the perfect family or the perfect past; not an ideal weight, or some specific amount of intelligence or artistic sensibility. If we are happy simply to be, that's the answer. We will attract happiness and happy situations to us, without effort and without struggle.

I open to the fountain of happiness within me.
I have everything I need.

April 22

Smile, breathe, and go slowly.
—Thich Nhat Hanh

We forget about our breath. We take it for granted. We rarely pause long enough, or expend the necessary consciousness, to focus on the air within us as it travels down the length of our spine like a wave, ebbing and flowing all day and night like the tide. Because we forget about it, we shorten its path. We breathe shallowly, in chops instead of waves, and suffer for the lack of distance. We miss out on the well-being and rejuvenation that are available to us.

The breath has the power to assist us. It increases our strength on the exhale and increases our relaxation as it fills us up on the inhale. It expands and contracts us in balance. It is release of tension and relief from pain, from anxiety, exhaustion, and suffocation. It is life force. It is meditation. It is health. Let's remember it. Let's remember to breathe fully and deeply, smoothly and with rhythm. Let's take advantage of our body's best medicine for calming and healing on the one hand, and for intense power and stamina on the other.

> *I breathe with gratitude and awareness.*
> *The rhythm of my breath heals me.*

April 23

Where a man feels pain he lays his hand.
—Dutch proverb

We want doctors to fix us, but they have their limits. The recipe for our ultimate healing has to come from the physician within. Medical professionals can put us back together when we break, and medicate our symptoms, and put us through a series of tests and protocols, but after they have done what they can do for us, sooner or later we have to face our own health and take responsibility for it.

We think that it's possible for something external to correct whatever ails us and that we can be made well forever, but it doesn't work like that. Health is a state of mind as well as body, a condition resulting from our choices and habits, so how we feel is largely up to us. This is good news! We have power within us. No matter what state of health we are in, no matter where we begin, we can help ourselves to feel better. We can always help ourselves to feel better.

I accept the limitations of doctors
and look within to improve the quality of my health.

April 24

Turn your wounds into wisdom.
—OPRAH WINFREY

We have all had a hard run of it in life. We have suffered injury, losses, abuse, neglect, betrayal, and heartbreak. We have felt worthless, and puffed up with pride. It is all this "stuff" that makes us human, and these are the realities of human life. But happily, because we have all suffered in our own ways, we can relate to each other.

Our misfortunes and grief do not separate us, as we may fear, but actually bring us together, and connect us deeply. Because we have lived through whatever horrors we have experienced, and survived them, we all have something of value to share. We do not have to let our hardships isolate us. There is always someone who knows how it feels.

And maybe we can even learn to laugh at our defense mechanisms and fears and avoidance strategies. Maybe we can learn to graciously accept the pitfalls of being human and find a way to be at peace with our vulnerability.

I am not alone in my suffering. As I suffer, so do we all.

*Being considerate of others will take your children further in life
than any college degree.*
—MARIAN WRIGHT EDELMAN

To be aware of those around us and consider what they might appreciate, and then act on it, is meaningful beyond measure. To be thoughtful, to not splatter our mess all over the place, to keep our part in things neat and tidy—these are behaviors that make us a pleasure to be around, and that bring love and appreciation raining down upon us.

The opposite behavior is tiresome. Unlike consideration, which is an ever-delightful surprise, inconsideration is a burr in our craw. It's exasperating. It's unbecoming. It's the height of selfishness. To expect others to clean up after us, and deal with our inefficiencies and misplacements without losing their cool, is unreasonable. It's enough to take care of ourselves without having to make allowances and exceptions for those who do not. Let's be considerate. Let's be a source of pleasure to others and not frustration. We will feel better, and so will they.

> *I clean up after myself and take the time
> to be considerate of others.*

April 26

They are as sick that surfeit with too much
as they that starve with nothing.
—SHAKESPEARE

No news is not always good news. For the person we are waiting to hear from, it may mean that we have lost our appeal. And too much news is no better. There is a kind of dependent sickness in constantly checking up and checking in. It feels fun at first, but wears thin.

Healthy balance in communication is the same as healthy balance elsewhere. It needs to be just right. Not enough communication feels like abandonment, and too much is suffocating.

We have built-in warning systems on both ends of the spectrum, but it's easy to ignore them. And though we may play at making no news after a certain point in time something other than disinterest, if it goes on too long, we are kidding ourselves. The no news is, in fact, its own *kind* of news. And we can pretend that too much communication is actually being meticulously attentive, but too much, in the end, is always too much.

I pay attention to signals of imbalance in communication,
and set appropriate boundaries and expectations.

We are all equally wise—and equally foolish.
—ALBERT EINSTEIN

We are not meant to serve the world as sacrificial lambs, sacrificing our needs and wants to those of our children, our spouses, our parents, bosses, or friends. Believing we don't matter, or that we are somehow *less* important than others, is ridiculous. No one is more important than we are, and we are no more important than anyone else. It's not a one or the other kind of proposition. We are all important. Our needs matter, and so do theirs. And there's a way to do the best we can by everyone, including ourselves. We can successfully compromise and negotiate. That's what compromise is for. We needn't habituate ourselves to martyrdom. It's neither recommended nor required.

Let's be well. Let's honor our needs, whatever they may be, and equally honor the needs of those we love.

> *There is room in life for everyone's needs to be met.*
> *Melodramatic sacrifice isn't necessary.*

April 28

What goes up must come down.
—Isaac Newton

Some days dawn bright and crisp, and our energy is lively and excitable. It feels good to be alive. We are happy to go to work, or to do whatever is before us. We have a sense of well-being, just because we do. And then, some days are flat and stale, right from the get-go. It's hard to wake up, and the journey of hours stretching before us seems long and difficult. We don't feel capable of the effort we know we will have to make. Even if we have a willing attitude on such days, the body's energy is sometimes just not there. Maybe it's burnout, or maybe it's just life.

Nothing is better than to feel good, to feel enthusiastic and energized. But it can't all be glorious. It's not meant to be. We can learn to roll with whatever the day brings, knowing that whatever we're *not* feeling is likely just around the corner. So if we're willing to wait for just a bit, then we will have it all!

> *I accept that everything comes easily on some days,*
> *and that other days require more effort.*

April 29

The Body says: I am a fiesta.
—EDUARDO GALEANO

Every body has its particular way of expressing itself. Some bodies speak in wiggles, some in angles, and some in curves and length. Our bodies have their own kind of personalities. They like certain movements, and styles of touch, and stretches, and they feel discomfort and aversion toward other things.

Finding the language of our body is a vital part of self-discovery. Understanding the joy of strength, and stature, and extension, and grace, as it suits *us* specifically, guarantees a life of healthy physical function and a happy body that feels honored and appreciated.

I honor my body, and tune in to discover the way it loves to move.

April 30

In the universe of possibility, you set the context and let life unfold.
—BENJAMIN ZANDER

Impossible things happen every day. We are sure that we don't have enough money, or luck, or experience, or savvy, or style, and yet we manage to accomplish unheard-of things and survive against all odds. Believing in what's possible comes first. We don't have to understand, or know, or figure anything out. We simply have to keep our minds and our hearts open. If we can do this, we will be blessed many times over, and then again.

Traditionally, we think small. We sell ourselves short. We believe only in what we can see and feel, and what we know for sure. But there is a whole other world at work that we cannot see. If we are truly open to all possibilities, the sky is the limit. Anything can happen, and does. It makes for good living, a boatload of gratitude, and blessings galore.

I am open to possibility. I believe that anything can happen, even if I don't understand how.

May 1

Do everything quietly and in a calm spirit. Do not lose your inner peace
for anything whatsoever, even if your whole world seems upset.
—St. Francis de Sales

I am occasionally prone to explosive little fits of temper. I feel the inconveniences of life, and things not going just my way, to be some kind of personal affront. And on occasion, I see others responding to life in the same way. It puts us in such a snippy and petulant place, and is so entirely unnecessary. Our temper tantrums don't change anything about circumstances and only make us angry and edgy and full of hatred. It's not worth it, not for one second.

Let's get better and better at not indulging our bad moods and disappointments. Why do we expect life to be so easy? If it were, it would hardly be satisfying. Our challenges help us grow. So let's learn to take the good with the bad and the bad with the good, and find a way to maintain our equilibrium the best we can throughout the ride.

I feel myself amping up into a fit of temper, and stop before I get
there. I remember that life is not supposed to be challenge-free.
I can stay calm in spite of whatever goes wrong.

May 2

Nature does not hurry, yet everything is accomplished.
—LAO TZU

Work smarter, not harder. That's never been my forte. The concept of expending less energy and achieving greater results I understand in theory, but my instinct and nature are beaver-like. I chew and build, and chew and build, and am busy, busy, busy ... always hard at work.

I seem to believe that the harder I work, the more worthwhile whatever I'm working toward will turn out to be, but I'm not entirely sure of the truth of that. There's something about the energy of pushing and striving and going hard at things that seems antithetical to finding peace and happiness.

Maybe hard work doesn't have to be hard. Maybe it's all about our approach. We can be strong and steady and purposeful and consistent, but we needn't be straining and uncomfortable. Work, in the end, is designed so that we might contribute our special talents to life, and to fulfill us deeply. It's not meant to strip us of every possible thing we have to give.

I take the strain out of my work effort.
I can be effective without being self-destructive.

May 3

It's what you learn after you know it all that counts.
—HARRY S. TRUMAN

Most of us have a smart aleck within. We think we can figure things out on our own without needing to follow directions. We feel certain that we can launch right into anything and be an expert, that we don't have to start at the beginning and build up. Other people have to do that, but not us. We can start in the middle, or even at the end.

By being so certain of ourselves when there is no legitimate basis for our certainty, we miss out on layers of intricacy and understanding. Maybe we even injure ourselves. Thinking we're above the need for help is a dangerous place to be. It invites disaster. If we don't right-size ourselves, the universe will do it for us.

Let's be okay with needing help and instruction, with not knowing and not understanding. If we must assume, let's assume that we don't know everything. That is the place to begin, and the only one that will ensure us of our ultimate success.

I can be a beginner at things.
I'm not afraid to ask questions and seek direction.

May 4

Character is much easier kept than recovered.
—THOMAS PAINE

Are loyalty and fidelity different things? Can we have one without the other? I have been told that this is a European concept: that loyalty is prized above fidelity. It doesn't feel on the level to me. It feels like justification for slippery behavior, and reminds me of times in my life when I have been told—reassured even—that what is clearly one thing is actually something else entirely. I have been made to feel like a fool for believing in what is evident and in what I see with my own eyes.

Let's choose to live with honor. It's blissfully guilt-free. Let's be scrupulous and morally meticulous and have integrity through and through. Let's be exactly what we are, and put a low value on pretension and lame excuses. If we don't hold ourselves to some kind of code of conduct, no one else will either.

I choose to live with honor and integrity.

I don't want to make money, I just want to be wonderful.
—MARILYN MONROE

If I have the right attitude, I can experience money and all of my financial fears and obligations almost playfully. Money comes in and money goes out. It ebbs and flows like the tides, sometimes a trickle and sometimes a rush, but always moving one way or the other. That's its only guarantee.

We want to arrest money and hold it captive and demand that it stay, but it evaporates in the misty night like a ghost and arrives in a whirlwind. It teases us, and we get frustrated. We want assurances, but money wants to play. We can learn to play along and laugh at the game, or suffer indefinitely from pushing against something that is ultimately as evasive as smoke.

> *I approach money matters with a sense of humor*
> *and don't let the dollar drag me down.*

May 6

*If you know you are on the right track, if you have this inner knowing,
then nobody can turn you off...no matter what they say.*
—BARBARA MCCLINTOCK

Sometimes things just feel right in a solid kind of way. We find ourselves calm beyond reason when we would expect to be giddy with excitement. We are reassured, and relax at a deep and inexplicable level. We somehow know that we are on track, and that everything is as it should be. It's as if we suddenly wake up from a fog and know beyond the shadow of a doubt that we really can trust in our path and the validity of our dreams.

I feel calm and steady when I am on track.

May 7

Certain flaws are necessary for the whole.
It would seem strange if old friends lacked certain quirks.
—GOETHE

We all have our pile of fears and insecurities, and I am willing to bet that at the bottom of most piles is the big fear that we are somehow not enough: not good enough, thin enough, smart enough, rich enough, pretty enough, or deserving enough. And we think that it's our job to become more of whatever we lack. We want to be more of *everything* to solve our problems. We suffer deeply from a consuming dis-ease of more.

But what if the real truth is that who we are and what we have are just right and absolutely perfect? What if we are missing our blessings and our gifts and talents by being too fiercely critical? Let's slow down and remember that who we are is deeper than what is on the surface, and deeper than our fears and judgments. Who we are is immeasurably beautiful, and who we are is just who we are supposed to be.

> *I appreciate the depth of my being*
> *and celebrate the wonder of who I am.*

May 8

The years teach much which the days never know.
—RALPH WALDO EMERSON

In general, when people reach a certain age of maturity, there is a kind of purity about them. Older folks who are in decent physical and mental health are positively twinkly. They are beyond the rush and fret of youth, beyond anxiety, beyond resistance, and largely beyond fear. They seem easily and naturally settled into present-moment awareness, and they have learned how to take their time. They are all about easy does it and good humor, and are amused at all of our youthful follies and self-imposed urgencies. They inspire us. They seem to have learned that in life, as in nature, everything is accomplished in its own sweet time.

I learn from my bright-eyed elders.
Life may not be as arduous as it sometimes seems.

May 9

Even nectar is poison if taken to excess.
—HINDU PROVERB

I value my solitude, but I can spend only so much time by myself before it starts to become unhealthy. My mind is busy, and noisy, and not always friendly. It tells me things. I value leisure time, but I can do *it* for only so long. I feel the lack of productivity. Too much relaxation makes me restless, and I look forward to getting back to work. But too much work depletes me ...

Everything in balance is the rule, and everything in moderation. I can only sleep so much, work so much, play so much, talk so much, listen so much, and cry so much. Too much of anything is simply too much.

I discover where there is too much of something in my life, and tip it in the opposite direction to restore balance.

May 10

You accept everybody just because they're alive and human.
—ALBERT ELLIS

There's savory and unsavory, in food, in the human character, and in the way we choose to live. What we create and surround ourselves with becomes our experience. If we are wholesome, we attract wholesome and live wholesome, and the same goes for seedy. And if we are one, and encounter the other, it can't help but rattle us a bit. When wholesome encounters seedy, there is a creepy darkness that spills over one way, and an unfamiliar, perhaps even detestable, freshness that spills over the other.

In cities of all kinds, both things live side by side, and immunity develops, but if we pluck anyone from the comfort zone they regularly inhabit and place them in the opposite environment, they will squirm. It's good to know where we live, but to be able to float among the other side on occasion, with our compassion and our curiosity leading the way, instead of our judgment. The earth, with her great generosity, carries and sustains us all.

> *I can be kind to people even if their choice*
> *of lifestyle makes me squirm.*

May 11

Life itself is the proper binge.
—JULIA CHILD

We are hungry beings—hungry for answers, for sweets, for love, for understanding, and for all that we lack. We are hungry for different bodies, different lives, and for a certain amount of blood and glory. We are hungry for *more* of everything: more money, more time, more sleep, more joy, more patience, and more freedom. We are insatiable. And we stuff ourselves with food and addictions and bad habits, whatever we can find.

But our appetite is endless, and nothing external abates it, not really, and definitely not permanently. We quest daily for satisfaction, and to determine finally and absolutely just what we need … to be happy … and full. But the only thing that really fills us is realizing that everything we need we already have. It's inside us. It's in gratitude, and acceptance, and integrity. Our salvation and happiness are as close as the moment, as close as our self-honesty, and as close as the satisfaction of a deep breath.

External grasping cannot ever satisfy my longing.
Fulfillment is an inside job.

May 12

Love must be as much a light as a flame.
—HENRY DAVID THOREAU

I love the smell of wet leaves. I love chilly mornings and the feel of the fresh air. I love breezes stirring tree leaves and having the best husband on earth. I love clouds in a blue sky and getting into bed after a long day. I love candlelit dinners and screened-in porches. I love to laugh and the telling of stories. I love the mountains and the vulnerability of people.

I love hope and joy and inspiration. I love being strong, and I love the flow of words on a page. I love the smell of bacon cooking, the taste of coffee, the color of vegetables, and hugging our German shepherd, Boss. I love the early morning and the late night, the afternoon, and the evening. I love feeling cozy, and I love feeling amped-up.

Giving expression to the things we love lifts us up. It's simple, and satisfying. Let's make it a regular practice to improve the quality of our lives!

I tell myself and others all the things I love about my life.

May 13

*The future is an opaque mirror. Anyone who tries to look into it
sees nothing but the dim outlines of an old and worried face.*
—Jim Bishop

It's so easy to project disaster all over our future. We are good at
thinking of everything that could go wrong, and making contingency plans in advance. We worry and stress out, thinking that
will give us some kind of control, but it doesn't.

Things rarely end up the way we think they will, and that's a
good thing. It's not our job to figure life out ahead of time. We
don't have to know how we will feel if this happens, or that. It *is*
our job to be a good sport and show up for the adventure with an
open mind and a positive attitude, and to enjoy every little bit of
the journey, however it may unfold.

I stop trying to figure out my future and enjoy the present instead.

May 14

As long as habit and routine dictate the pattern of living,
new dimensions of the soul will not emerge.
—HENRY VAN DYKE

We are not as complicated as we think we are. Fundamental patterns circle over and over and round and about in our lives. They scare us. They motivate us. They inspire us, and put us on the defensive. They form the scaffolding of our entire belief system, and give structure and background to all of our actions.

Let's take the time to learn these patterns and understand where they come from, to bring ever higher awareness to why we do what we do. That way, we can change the things that don't serve us any longer and refine the things that do. Whether we are conscious of our patterns or not, they operate on every level of our lives, so maybe it's worth it to take the time and make the effort to look at them. Maybe becoming conscious of these patterns is in some way the whole point of our lives.

I identify patterns in the way I behave, and in order to behave
better, I am willing to change.

May 15

She never quite leaves her children at home,
even when she doesn't take them along.
—Margaret Culkin Banning

It's an incredible thing to be a mother. In some ways, it's the most heart-wrenching experience on earth, from the high hopes and physical strangeness of pregnancy, with its fears and heartburn and labor pains, to the absolute terror of taking the newly born and entirely too-tiny baby home. And that's just the beginning. Motherhood is a labor of love from the deepest core of loving, love from the nerves and heart and intestines.

And it's the same for the one who mothered us, and the mothering of ourselves as well. Let's be grateful for all of it. It's an endless journey of growing up. The lessons may not always come in the style of Norman Rockwell, but motherhood as it is, with all of its joys and sorrows, is magnificent and beautiful beyond measure.

Today I honor motherhood in all of its manifestations
and the incredible gift of life.

May 16

In three words I can sum up everything I've learned about life: it goes on.
—ROBERT FROST

A sense of well-being is a treat. It is generally a fleeting thing, coming and going like a breeze, or a bird. Some mornings we just wake up and feel good. We have a sense that all is well and that we needn't worry, that abundance and joy abound. Our bodies are unusually pain-free and we are happy to be up and at 'em. And then, some mornings require more effort. We are heavy with the unknown, and afraid and uncomfortable. We are restless and frantic.

We feel amazing. We feel horrible. We feel certain. We are filled with doubt. Our feelings cycle like the sun. So when we *do* feel good, let's recognize it and be sure to enjoy it. Let's appreciate feelings of peace. Let's be glad and be grateful, knowing that sensations of well-being, like all sensations, must pass.

I fully enjoy my moments of well-being. It feels good to feel good!

May 17

No price is too high to pay for the privilege of owning yourself.
—FRIEDRICH NIETZSCHE

I don't want to miss anything. I don't want to be left out. I want to be included and invited and to be a part of whatever is happening. It might be interesting. It might be fun. Some great, unexpected challenge or adventure might ensue ... and I want to be there for it. I want to be there for all of the little details and soft moments, the laughter, the tension, the road trip. Plus, I want my time alone. I need regular, reflective time in solitude. And I have found that wanting it all sometimes creates a conflict in me. Maybe I want too much!

By necessity, I am learning to be okay wherever I am and whatever I am doing and to make peace with my choices, to fully accept my "yes, pleases" and "no, thank yous." I am beginning to trust that my path will lead me exactly where I am supposed to go, and that if I miss a turn somehow, it must have been the wrong one ... for me.

I don't ever have to feel left out. I trust that whatever
I experience is exactly what I am supposed to experience.

May 18

We must embrace pain and burn it as fuel for our journey.
—KENJI MIYAZAWA

Why do bad things happen to good people? Why do bad things happen at all? Why is there suffering on earth? Why is there pain? How do we make sense of it? We grow through hardship. Maybe that is why. We realize things. We learn to apologize and forgive. We learn to appreciate peace and joy and all of the good things that we *do* have.

I believe that challenge is opportunity. It is a call to evolve. With care and attention, we can transform pain into blessing and suffering into love. It's possible and it's worth it. Scar tissue is stronger than any other, and our wounds make us beautiful. Whatever we may face, let's choose the spiritual lesson instead of bitter revenge.

I understand that pain and suffering are gifts to grow my spirit, and I am bigger and brighter for all that I go through.

Anger is a wind which blows out the lamp of the mind.
—ROBERT G. INGERSOLL

There is so much anger in the world. People are like hair triggers. The smallest thing sets them off. Explosively, violently, they lash out. They glare with hatred as they pass us in their cars. We are not going fast enough, or they otherwise disapprove of our driving style. They blast their horns. They loudly and publicly reprimand cashiers, servers, children, and their spouse.

Let's not be one of them. Let's not spew anger like knives. Let's shine a light of love instead. Let's keep our sense of humor. And if we cannot, if we feel uncontrollably hostile, let's stop blaming the world and look within. That is where both our issues and our answers reside.

I forgive those who lash out in anger
and carefully monitor my own irritability to keep it in check.

May 20

Dare to be true.
—GEORGE HERBERT

Most of us think we are more honest than we really are. We fool ourselves with our justifications and our excuses. We talk ourselves into believing whatever we *want* to believe. The truth is often hard to face. It requires that we undress emotionally, that we admit that we are afraid, wrong, mistaken, that we may have been cruel. Self-honesty requires us to be vulnerable. We have to confess our imperfection to offer or receive forgiveness.

But the other side of such honesty is heart-opening relief and freedom from shame. Being willing to expose our vulnerability is well worth the courage it takes.

I stop pretending and get honest with myself.

May 21

All differences in this world are of degree, and not of kind,
because oneness is the secret of everything.
—SWAMI VIVEKANANDA

That we are "all one" is a spiritual concept that is hard to get a grip on. What does it mean? That we are the same? That we are connected by our being human and having human feelings and issues? That what I do to you I somehow do to myself?

This concept is an intellectual puzzle, and I find myself wanting to figure it out. But I don't really think figuring has anything to do with it. I think this concept has to do with energy and love and a heart so full of compassion that it aches. It's opening to the divine essence within us that we all share: the flame of life, our spirit, our core. We are connected deeply. And all any of us want, really, is to love and be loved.

I am kind and accepting with everyone, myself included.
We are all aching with love.

May 22

I guess you can tease me about being a drama queen,
because that did heighten the drama.
—GREG LOUGANIS

Even if big things are happening, life doesn't have to be full of high drama. It can be calm and proceed steadily, no matter what, if *we* are calm and proceed steadily. The currents of our lives reflect us. If we are frantic, we feel anxious. If we are defensive, we feel angry. If we are always in a rush, we feel harried.

If, on the other hand, we take whatever happens in stride, and trust in the ultimate goodness of our path, we needn't fly off the handle at every little thing. We can keep our cool and live drama-free.

I consider my part in creating the drama of my life,
and make changes in the way I behave to minimize the drama.

May 23

*Nowhere can man find a quieter or more untroubled retreat
than in his own soul.*
—MARCUS AURELIUS

In some ways, loneliness is more a state of mind than a physical reality. We can feel lonely in crowds, lonely in marriages, and lonely with a group of friends. We can feel like no one understands us, or cares, and that we are so alone.

But we're not alone. Not really. We are connected to others at our very source, and at any time, in any way, we can step into the middle of life and make friends and make connections and make room for others in our hearts. We can listen to someone who needs to talk. We can tell someone what's going on with us. Getting out of loneliness is a question of changing our mind. It's learning to think about what we can give, and what we can share, and how we can contribute, instead of thinking about what we're not getting. The irony is that when we give it, we get it!

If I am feeling lonely, I go out in the world and interact with people. I think about what I have to offer, and I offer it!

May 24

All which we behold is full of blessings.
—WILLIAM WORDSWORTH

Gratitude is one of the most powerful tools for transmuting darkness into light, depression into gladness, lethargy into enthusiasm, and hatred into love. It can begin with something simple: I am grateful for the way the bathroom rug feels on my bare feet in the morning. And it snowballs easily. I am grateful for green tea, or coffee, as the case may be. I am grateful for breakfast, for my commercial-free radio, for the fact that my car starts and runs and is pretty good on gas. I am grateful that I *have* a car. I am grateful that I have a job. I am grateful for sunny days and warm breezes and blooming flowers in the spring. I am grateful that I am becoming more flexible in every way as I get older. I am grateful that I believe in possibility, that I see the beauty in most people, and that I can laugh more easily than I once could. Articulating gratitude expands the joy in my life. There is always something. Endless blessings surround me on all sides if I only open my heart to them.

I am aware of my blessings and express my gratitude.

May 25

Fill what's empty. Empty what's full. And scratch where it itches.
—ALICE ROOSEVELT LONGWORTH

What constitutes "just right"? Finding the proper balance has been, and continues to be, a journey. Perhaps there is no fixed answer. Life is a constant tidal flow, filling and emptying, emptying and filling, never one absolutely, or the other, but a give and take, a continuous process of adding and subtracting. I can add a new habit to my routine. I can add a chair to a room. I can stop overreacting. I can get rid of the rug that is fraying at the edges and trips me every time I walk across it. I can recognize that I am spending too much time alone, or not enough. I can adjust and adapt. I can tune in and take a reading, understanding that there is no fixed position and there is no final point of arrival. Everything is adjustment and correction, and everything is forever in flux.

What do I need more of in my life today? And what can I let go of? I am willing to make the necessary changes to equalize the balance.

May 26

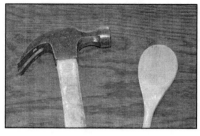

It's not what you are that holds you back, it's what you think you are not.
—DENIS WAITLEY

Who determines how much we are worth? Because I am a better cook than I am a carpenter, does that mean I am worth more in a kitchen than I am in a woodshop? Or is there something deeper to me? A more intrinsic kind of impossible-to-measure value? Is my worth determined by the attention I get? Or the people who love me? Or how much money I make? Or by my car or my physical beauty? Are some people more worthy than others? And if so, why?

I can discount myself any time I want to, and I can allow others to discount me as well, or I can go the other way and inflate myself. But ideally, I am neither puffed up nor deflated. Ideally, I am just right as I am. Depending on where I set my boundaries and how abused I allow myself to be, I can be bright and priceless or I can be enslaved and pathetic. So how much am I worth? Maybe the best answer is that I am as worthy as I consider myself to be in any given situation. I am as worthy as I feel.

It's up to me to establish my worth.

May 27

*The legacy of heroes is the memory of a great name
and the inheritance of a great example.*
—BENJAMIN DISRAELI

Let us honor the fight for freedom today. Let us honor those who have fallen and all those who have served. Let us honor the memory of our own life's battles as well, and the veteran that lives in all of us. Let us feel grateful for this day, and for courage and heroes and victory and surrender. Let us express our appreciation for the peace we so readily enjoy.

I am grateful for my freedom.

May 28

Change always comes bearing gifts.
—PRICE PRITCHETT

Because of our fear of the future, we often fail to make a change, choosing instead to stick with what we know, even if it's not working for us. But there is reward in stepping forth with courage. There is renewal and revival. It's worth it. Absolutely.

Even small changes can add vitality to life: driving an adventurous route through an unknown part of town, ordering something new when eating out, dressing with inspired style, signing up for a workshop, starting to exercise, taking a risk. Let's enjoy the curious wonder that comes from a fresh way of going about things.

I welcome the fresh air of change into my life.

May 29

Smooth seas do not make skillful sailors.
—AFRICAN PROVERB

When confronted with a task I'm unsure of, I'm skeptical right off the bat. I consider it critically and with a certain sense of inner whining. How am I supposed to do *that*? It feels overwhelming, impossible. I'm not sure how to begin. Every part of me wants to turn away and not face it, not do it. And my negativity actually fuels the first attempt at combat, which is what it is at first: me against the job. I fumble and curse. I sweat. I approach it clumsily from one side and then another.

And somewhere along the way, I realize that in all of my awkwardness I have actually made progress, and hope flickers. I begin to understand what's required and how I might be more efficient. I stop cursing and start engaging my creativity. I cease to struggle and slowly shift toward acceptance. The job gets done, and when it's over, I feel satisfied that I faced what I did not want to face and accomplished something worth accomplishing. I overcame my own resistance.

I trust that a seemingly impossible job
will get easier if I only begin.

May 30

We need not destroy the past. It is gone.
—JOHN CASE

Things bubble up in life and we are forced to deal with happenings from our past. They come up when we are ready to face them, when we can understand and process them, and when we're ready to let them go. As such, it's useful to go rooting around in the past, but the trick is to do so with limits and purpose and to not get stuck there. Focusing too much of our energy on the past can be a potentially dangerous proposition. Hunting for self-pity and excuses in our history serves as a present-day responsibility cop-out.

All of our real answers, all hope for happiness and all fulfillment and joy, are right here, in the present moment. Going back in any way, either wistfully or with an investigative air, cannot fundamentally satisfy our needs and longings. Only the present moment can do that.

I stay where I am and appreciate the now.

May 31

Be proud to wear you.
—Dodinsky

Life is a continuous process of befriending ourselves. We are so changeable and fragile. A stranger's comment, a pang of self-consciousness or embarrassment, an unbecoming reflection in the mirror, or a few pounds in the wrong direction on the scale can completely topple our self-assurance. We must be compassionate, and honest about what we are feeling. A bit of gentle coaxing and sympathy for ourselves goes a long way toward easing the pressure for perfection and the desire to blame others for our discomfort.

And then we can make the changes we need to make, or have a good cry, or ask for help, or spend some time peacefully in solitude. We can give ourselves the time and space that we need for healing. Simply allowing ourselves to be where we are is a huge relief.

I am willing to give myself a break today.
I allow myself to be exactly where I am.

June 1

See everything; overlook a great deal; correct a little.
—Pope John XXIII

We rarely take the time to understand another person's point of view, and as a general rule, we are not particularly good listeners. It takes less effort to make others wrong than to ask questions and search for common ground, though the common ground does exist. We all have our gifts and our personal fears. We all have less than honorable motivations at times and the ability to harshly judge. But judgment backfires. It makes for an interior world of suspicion and criticism, and we block ourselves from the soothing and sustaining warmth of love.

Just for today, let's leave judgment alone. Let's not take on the judgment of others and feel resentful and misunderstood, and let's not slap our own opinions all over those whom we encounter. Let's live today in a spirit of acceptance and tolerance and forgiveness. Just for today, let's live and let live.

I accept others with their limitations and imperfections,
and I accept myself the same way.

June 2

No one can get inner peace by pouncing on it.
—HARRY EMERSON FOSDICK

Relaxation is the ability to enjoy what *is*, exactly as it is. It is the release of pressure that has built up in us over the unknown future or what remains undone in our day. It is the art of receiving what's in front of us, whether it be a sunny highway filled with traffic, or a friend struggling with her own life issues, or a summer evening on a porch swing with a breeze.

Our culture does not encourage relaxation, though it pushes and forces it on us with aggressive solutions and suggestions. Relax! It becomes almost a demand, like standing in a field and calling loudly for wild animals to come to us. It doesn't happen that way. We must get quiet and wait calmly. We have to create spaciousness within to allow for relaxation within. It is an internal emotional cease-fire. It's a letting go and surrender. It's trusting in the process of life and the journey we are on, taking in the sights with all of our curiosity and wonder, and remembering and appreciating what a beautiful adventure this is.

I am willing to let go today and invite the energy of relaxation inside.

June 3

God gives us dreams a size too big so that we can grow into them.
—AUTHOR UNKNOWN

Big life projects are too big to digest at once. We can break them down into small bites, and easily accomplish piecemeal what seems impossible to do all at once. And that's how all of life happens anyway, isn't it? One small effort at a time, one day at a time? It's possible to overextend and go beyond comfort to the point of pain and distraction, to live on nerves and on edge, and to teeter indefinitely at the end of our ropes. But what does that prove?

It is appropriate and healthy to feel satisfied with bite-sized accomplishments in the direction of the bigger picture and be pleased with reasonable, steady progress. We get a lot more done that way, and enjoy the doing of it all the more.

I take my time today and stop the rush and the push.
I enjoy making reasonable efforts in the right direction
and feel the satisfaction of steady, sustainable progress.

June 4

The light is all.
—RALPH WALDO EMERSON

I find changing light to be soothing. I am carried by the angles of the sun and shadows; by dawn and light rising, the morning glare shifting seamlessly into the noontime blast, and then the slow progression back into softness as the sun lowers and the afternoon idles away. My body lets go one level at a time as the day's brightness dissolves into the comfort of dusk and the cover of darkness.

Revolving suns and moons are a blessing and a source of renewal. I am grateful for all of the continuous and subtle shifts in light. They remind me that we are all shifting and cycling, eternally, from brightness to dusk, from crisp freshness to murky mist, and from noontime to midnight. We are directly related to the cycles of the sky. We reflect each other. And the sunrise always comes.

I will bring awareness to the light today,
and appreciate the way it moves and changes.

June 5

Stress is poison.
—AGAVÉ POWERS

If we are stressed-out, on edge, and rigid with pressure, we spread tension. If we are relaxed, easy to laugh, serene, secure, and at ease, others feel good in our presence. If I am not feeling it—if I am hungry, angry, tired, or sore—then perhaps just by acknowledging the way I feel I can minimize my negative impact on others. I can send out a warning flag of information: "I feel grouchy. I need to eat something." The alternative is to unconsciously bark and sigh and complain and abuse, maybe even allowing ourselves to believe that someone else is responsible for our ill behavior and that our foulness is somehow their fault.

Let's recognize the impact of our moods and our energy. Let's be honest about the fact that the way we are affects everything and everyone around us. If we snap or are darkly moody, let's make every effort to catch ourselves and change our approach. We have a role in how we feel and the space we occupy. Let's choose to spread joy!

I am willing to be cheerful and pleasant today.

June 6

What a wonderful life I've had! I only wish I'd realized it sooner.
—COLETTE

We all think, if only this and if only that, *then* I could be happy. And sometimes we get what we think we want, and lo and behold, it does not make us happy. So we look out again and think of something else. It must be that other thing, that thing over there. *That's* what will make me happy. But it won't, and it can't, because happiness is not generated from the outside. It's something that arises inside of us. And once we tap into it, we no longer require expensive toys or fancy houses, or to be popular or wildly successful or whatever it is. We are simply happy to be alive and to experience whatever is in front of us.

Happiness is a state of mind and a way of being. It is not something we can achieve or capture. It is something we already are, and if we want to experience it, we must open to it and allow it. It is simple pleasure. It is a cup of tea, a glass of cold water, a smile from across the room, a hot summer evening, the feeling of soft sheets, views of mountains, and a job well done.

I open to happiness today, and simple pleasures.
I am okay within myself. I am happy.

June 7

Try to become not a man of success,
but try rather to become a man of value.
—ALBERT EINSTEIN

To me, a successful man or woman is one who has achieved a certain level of self-acceptance and a certain level of life acceptance, one who is peaceful inside, and kind, loving, forgiving, and compassionate. A successful man or woman can be counted on and is self-reflective, willing to change, able to see more than one side of things, open-minded, and open-hearted. Human success is about spiritual enlightenment, it seems to me, and not the accumulation of physical things. An angry and bitter man is not successful no matter how much money he has. And likewise, a man with peace in his heart is successful no matter how much money *he* has. We can be successful with or without money, with or without a big job, with or without a high level of education, but we cannot be successful without love in our hearts and kindness and integrity in our souls.

Insofar as I express love and kindness in my life, I am a success.

June 8

My own prescription for health is less paperwork
and more running barefoot through the grass.
—Terri Guillemets

Everything is evolution or maintenance, one or the other. We are either growing taller or growing stronger. Evolution gives us height, and maintenance gives us depth. If we do not take proper care of ourselves for a day, there is no great harm done. But stack up a number of days on top of each other and we will begin to suffer from declining energy, ill health, and erratic emotions. It's so much easier to keep up than to catch up.

Properly feeding ourselves, and moving and stretching our bodies, and relaxing, and fully expressing all that we have to express, are daily exercises. "Diet" in every sense of the word is a way of life. So let's commit to doing all the things that make us feel good on a regular basis. Let's be willing to expend some effort every day for the reward of good health.

I am willing to exercise myself daily in every way—
spiritually, mentally, emotionally, and physically—and the result
is my ability to experience exceptional health and joy in living.

June 9

If things go wrong, don't go with them.
—ROGER BABSON

We all worry and fret over things that are just around the corner. We are full of what ifs and wonderings. And then we turn the corner with rising trepidation, we pass the thing we fear, and we promptly drop it from our thoughts. We anticipate the next corner and fret anew.

But what if we didn't fret? What if we refused to get all twisted up? What if we decided not to worry at all? What if we considered that our personal path might be less about making it happen and more about letting it happen?

It's the surprises in life that make it life, and make it interesting, and make it fun. Let's trust in the future instead of being afraid of it, and trust in the surprises and the whole variety of happenings of our life.

> *I stop worrying about what may or may not*
> *happen tomorrow and enjoy today.*

June 10

Remember that everyone you meet is afraid of something,
loves something, and has lost something.
—H. JACKSON BROWN JR.

A firm handshake may be the best kind, but it's uncomfortable to be at the receiving end of an over-squeeze. Just so, if I shake firmly with someone who has a dead-fish hand, *I* am overpowering. Maybe the thing to do is to match the other: soggy for soggy, firm for firm. That's not the standard practice, but that's the nature of real "do unto others," it seems to me. Real compassion and kindness require a reading, a sensitivity, and a bit of creative imagination. It's not the thought that whomever I'm dealing with should appreciate what I'm doing because it's right or best, and what *I* would want, but rather to ask and consider the questions, What does *he* want? What does *she* want? What are the signals here, and how can I best be of service? Let's not thrust our own ideas of what's best on others, but listen and look for signs that tell us what would be most helpful, most needed, and most appreciated ... by them.

I pay attention to others today
and treat them the way they want to be treated.

June 11

There are two lasting bequests we can give our children:
One is roots. The other is wings.
—HODDING CARTER JR.

The parental journey is a mixed blessing. Our children grow up and find their independence as young adults, but we still are "home" to each other in a lasting kind of way. We don't "fit" anymore the way we once did, and we don't entirely approve of one other. There is suspicion and disbelief on both sides. It is their time to be out in the world exploring all of its features and having grand adventures and knowing everything, and it's our time to enjoy small, simple pleasures. To them, we are home port and a free meal, tolerable in small doses but essentially uninteresting.

We teeter together in the same home space, but look out in far different directions. And it's okay. We are right on time. It will shift again and again and again as the years carry us onward.

I respect the ways my children are different from me,
and I keep on loving them no matter what.

June 12

The willingness to share does not make one charitable; it makes one free.
—ROBERT BRAULT

Sometimes in restaurants I see couples who are together but do not seem to see each other. They do not speak except in monosyllables. Often one or both of them is distracted by a cell phone and more involved with the small electronic device in front of them than their living, breathing partner, the person they married, presumably because of common interests and great love between them. But no love is visible here, only barriers to love.

What opens people to people, no matter how strong the walls between them, is conversational sharing and the exposure of individual vulnerability. This is what's going on inside of me. Here's what I'm feeling and thinking. Here's what I'm afraid of and what I long for, and here are all of my insecurities. Such honesty allows the other to see us anew and reawakens love and compassion ... but it takes two who are willing. Open communication is not safe or possible with everyone, but where it is safe and possible, it is an exquisitely beautiful thing.

I am willing to listen with compassion and to share from my heart.

June 13

It is easier to be wise for others than for ourselves.
—Francois VI, duc de La Rochefoucauld

We love to give unsolicited advice. We love to make suggestions about all the ways people can improve their lives, and then feel shunned and even resentful if our suggestions aren't implemented. We think we know what's best and what's needed. And yet, if someone gives *us* unsolicited advice, we are offended. We feel condescended to, not trusted to make our own way, and annoyed that anyone should be so nosy. When other people interfere with us, they should mind their own business, but when we interfere with others, we are being helpful. Or are we?

Let's refrain from offering our opinions and pushing our helpful suggestions onto people and their life choices. If someone wants to know what we think or what we would do, chances are they will ask us. Then we can share our point of view. But once we share it, we have to leave it alone. What other people do with our thoughts and suggestions is up to them.

I mind my own business and keep my judgments
and opinions to myself.

June 14

The doors we open and close each day decide the lives we live.
—FLORA WHITTEMORE

"No" is a powerful and important word, and most of us are afraid to use it. We grow up thinking we are supposed to be everything to everybody all of the time. And if someone asks us to do something and we actually *can't* do it because of an unavoidable conflict, we apologize and possibly feel guilty.

But we are not meant to be doormats or lackeys. We are not meant to spend volumes of time pleasing other people and doing their bidding. We are not meant to consistently do more than our share. That's as distorted as doing nothing. The thing is to say yes when we mean yes, but not to say yes when we really want to say no. Each of us is a limited resource, and we must learn to protect and preserve ourselves. Otherwise, we burn out and become endangered, sick, and no good to anyone.

Without guilt or feelings of obligation,
I say yes when I mean yes, and no when I mean no.

June 15

Just because you're miserable doesn't mean you can't enjoy your life.
—ANNETTE GOODHEART

Some people get stuck, utterly stuck, in a wrong way of seeing that imprisons the spirit and blocks the light. We all know people like that, people living behind bars of their own making. And any of us would be hard-pressed to help them understand the situation they are in and free themselves. It's beyond them. They are too busy pointing fingers and blaming the world.

But even if they stay miserable, we can keep on loving these people and living in the light ourselves. We may not be able to bring them peace or show them their error, and we cannot make them see the world differently than they see it. That change has to come from inside of them. But we *can* have compassion and send out prayers and refuse to take ownership of the polluted thoughts they try to send our way. We can be pleasant, but we do need to stay on guard.

I believe that change is possible for even the darkest of souls,
but know that it doesn't happen for everyone.
I work on my own light and share the love I have.

June 16

Your body is a temple, but only if you treat it as one.
—ASTRID ALAUDA

Would we be entirely comfortable wearing a bathing suit in front of the people we work with? What about our extended family? How about our friends? Does it depend on the situation? I believe more people than not feel shy exposing their bodies to others, even if their bodies are beautiful. There's a vulnerability and uncertainty in revealing ourselves, in showing our weight and muscle. No matter what we look like, most of us seem to have body doubts.

Can we learn to wear our bodies with appreciation? Can we give thanks for our back, for our eyes and ears, our chest and ribs, our arms and legs, and our beating heart that pumps and pumps and pumps? Let's make an effort. Let's celebrate our flesh and bones! Just for today, let's be okay with our bodies just the way they are.

I have the courage to appreciate and accept my body as it is.

June 17

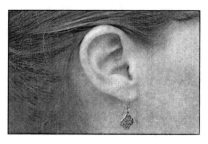

Listen or your tongue will keep you deaf.
—Native American proverb

If we are knowledgeable about a subject, it's difficult to sit back and let others speak when the topic is being discussed in a group. Something in us wants to be the expert, to blurt out information, and to appear wise. Something in us wants to take over. Perhaps we feel as if we must push and jockey for position and time and attention or our point of view will not have a chance.

When we finish other people's sentences, when we answer questions that have not even been completely asked, when we interrupt, we lose credibility. It's better to listen and wait, and consider. It's better to be responsive, not reactive. It's better to trust that there is time and space to explain the way we see things, and that we do not have to speak loudly and aggressively in order to be heard.

I listen completely to others and do not jump the gun in order to share my perspective. I relax and trust that there is time enough for all that needs to be said.

June 18

Perhaps the truth depends on a walk around the lake.
—WALLACE STEVENS

A walk is good for the soul as well as the body. It opens our mind and shifts our perspective. The fresh air releases tightness and discomfort that come from being sequestered too long indoors and sitting in cars. A walk is soothing and refreshing.

And walking doesn't have to be a long and arduous undertaking. It's not like jogging or "exercise," specifically, though some people think of it that way. It's simpler than that, and smaller. It's moving the body and stretching the legs, and opening to things beyond technology. It's a return to nature, even in the middle of the city. Fifteen minutes in the presence of the sky can change the quality of any day. In crisp winter as much as the heat, a walk is available to us. We need only answer our soul's call to get out and get moving, to enjoy the natural sights and sounds, and the fresh air, and the rhythm of our footsteps.

*I will make time for a walk outside today,
even if it's only for a few minutes. It opens my mind
and restores my soul. A walk reminds me of who I am.*

June 19

*There isn't a child who hasn't gone out into the brave new world
who eventually doesn't return to the old homestead
carrying a bundle of dirty clothes.*
—ART BUCHWALD

Being "cool" used to be about doing things that I wasn't supposed to do, and doing them with a certain brazen sense that I could somehow get away with them without having to suffer any consequences. I knew my choices were dangerous, but I chose them anyway. Being cool was saying "I dare you" to danger. I felt powerful and untouchable. I stood up and challenged life to slap me, and then, eventually, it did. The wake-up call always comes.

What's cool for me today is different. It's recognizing that consequences do happen and that I can work with them. No more pretending that I am bigger and badder than cause and effect. Being cool today is knowing who I am and refusing to pretend otherwise. It's working with the reality of my strengths and weaknesses to be the best and happiest me that I can be.

*I don't need to pretend to be anything.
There's nothing cooler than being authentically myself.*

June 20

Love is, above all, the gift of oneself.
—JEAN ANOUILH

We think that if we meet the *right* person, then that person will make us happy, take care of our needs and wants, and be our unending source of bliss. But this thinking is all wrong. We are responsible for our own happiness. It's not up to anyone else.

Instead of dependency, there is freedom in true love. Neither partner *needs* the other for completion or happiness. There is friendship and enjoyment and support that can be counted on. The relationship is a choice and a pleasure, not a duty. It is two whole people supporting each other as each pursues his or her own dreams and happiness. There is room for aspiration and growth and exploration of each partner individually and both partners together. The relationship is spacious and satisfying and is the *result* of self-acceptance and wholeness, not the cause.

> *I have to be happy with me before I can be happy*
> *in a relationship with someone else.*

June 21

Do not anticipate trouble or worry about what may never happen.
—BENJAMIN FRANKLIN

A worried state of mind gets us nothing worth having. It gives us gray hair and wrinkles and a sense of fear. We prepare for disappointment and disaster. We brace ourselves for certain horrors and try to prevent them from happening in advance. We make our plans and then we fret over all of the unlikely negative possibilities. But things often turn out better than we think they will. And even if things do go south, they rarely go wrong in the way we expect.

What if, like a child waiting for a surprise from a loving parent, we expect good things in our future, instead of trials and stressors and punishment? What if we trust that no matter what happens, it will somehow end up blessing us, and what if, no matter how chaotic or disastrous a situation appears, we trust that it has come to teach us something that will ultimately result in our happiness or our ability to better cope with life? Let's have faith that way. Let's free ourselves from the stress and angst of worry.

Worrying is not worth my time or effort.
I trust the future and let go of my fear.

June 22

He who trims himself to suit everyone will soon whittle himself away.
—Raymond Hill

It can be a crush to my ego to hear through the grapevine what other people—people who don't know me—think about me, to get the bird's-eye view of the way I am perceived from a distance. I always find it startling. The external perception is so different from the way I know myself to be. I can't even begin to know all of the people who have opinions about me, and I certainly can't control the way everyone thinks. It bothers me that people misperceive me, but it seems ridiculous to resist it. I cannot change the way I am. It's best, perhaps, to quietly carry the knowledge that if they knew me better, they would perceive me differently.

Let's take a moment to consider the way we form opinions about others from a distance. We must have volumes of our own misperceptions as well. Let's make an effort and make a decision to give people a break. We all have a soft underbelly, and none of us can possibly be as rugged or tough or pathetic or callous as we might seem.

> *I trust that we all have more depth and sensitivity*
> *than is immediately apparent.*

June 23

A good laugh and a long sleep are the best cures.
—IRISH PROVERB

I sometimes underestimate the effect of hunger and exhaustion on my spirits. If I am hungry, I feel on edge. I am shaky and irritable and almost frantic. Nothing is happening fast enough or the way I want it to. And physical and mental exhaustion are equally uncomfortable. I become overwhelmed to the point of despair. I feel as if there is just too much to do and I cannot possibly do it all. I feel drained and empty and frustrated. I am not very graceful about accepting my limitations. I want to be able to do everything and be everything and make time for everything, and to do it all without needing to eat or rest. I resist my own humanness.

But it's okay to have limits. There's no real percentage in pushing to the edge of the envelope and beyond. Going faster and farther and faster still, and filling my life and my days with more things and activities and more yet again, gets me nothing of value. I can make a better choice today. I can be kind to myself.

I accept my limitations and am okay with not being able to do it all.

June 24

Saying thank you is more than good manners. It is good spirituality.
—ALFRED PAINTER

I am grateful for my car. It transports me safely all over the earth and doubles as a complete and secure home away from home. I can park it in scenic spots and work on my computer, or recline the seat for a nap. It has perfect and necessary cubbies and containers for lip balm and hand lotion and coins for the tolls. I can listen to the radio, talk on the phone, say my prayers out loud, or sit in absolute silence with the road passing beneath the circling tires. There's usually no one in my car but me. It's my private and personal space.

What an incredible luxury that we can hop in our cars, turn a key, and go anywhere. Our cars mean freedom and adventure. The ones we choose and the way we keep them reflect our personalities. Our cars are so much more than rubber and steel. They deserve our appreciation. Without them, our lives would be smaller, and limited, and empty of beautiful roadside vistas.

I express my gratitude for my car today,
and recognize the incredible freedom it gives me.

June 25

A man's as miserable as he thinks he is.
—SENECA

Self-pity consumes all that it comes in contact with. It's dangerous and internally uncomfortable. It's a claiming of victim status. In self-pity, I have no responsibility, but only rights. I have the right to complain and be miserable and make others miserable because life is harder for me than anyone else. I am stretched to my limits but unwilling to stop. I have the desire to complain and no interest in the business of correcting what's wrong. I seem to want sympathy, but I don't really. I only want whining entitlement. You would, too, if your life was like mine. That's the way the thinking goes. It's stuck in the problem and has no interest in the solution.

While self-pity is blind and petty, its antithesis is visionary and abundant, and available with only a slight shift in perspective. All is well, all is possible, and blessings abound. If I am miserable, I have choices. I can stay miserable, or make the decision to change my mind.

I can pity myself for only so long. I am rich with blessings.

June 26

We dance round in a ring and suppose,
but the Secret sits in the middle and knows.
—ROBERT FROST

Love and health, hardship and reward, all ebb and flow like the tide. Goodness and joy swell in and out. Whitecaps of fear and anxiety ripple and fume. But below the fickle surface of waves and tides, flotsam and jetsam, is the deep, the quiet, and the source of all life. It is essence. It is inside each of us. We share it with all living things.

Beyond all the impermanence we experience, there is that which does not change. It sustains us and inspires us. It is the reason for everything, but it does not show itself in obvious ways. It beckons in our dreams and longings and it whispers to us to trust. It is love and life. It is all-encompassing freedom. It is readily available, but we must learn to pay attention.

I trust that I am bigger than the changing tides of my life.
I share a powerful connection with all that lives.

June 27

If you breathe well you will live long.
—SANSKRIT PROVERB

Breath is a wave that stimulates our spine and nerves. It is meant to travel from inhalation all the way down our vertebrae to the "sacred" sacral bone, and then travel back up. But sadly, most of us breathe no deeper than in our chest. Our range of air is from our nipples to our nose, and we rob ourselves of life force by chopping the breath in half.

Breath is power. Let's learn to take advantage of it. Like a roll of thunder, we can build a breath within us and bring it to the outside as a slow and solid force, or let it be a letting go and release of tension. Let's make an effort to breathe consciously. Let's breathe deeply and fluidly. Let's not waste our precious air in choppy hyperventilation.

I breathe fully today, with awareness and gratitude.

June 28

Look ... and if you have eyes you will be able to see
that the whole existence is joyful. Everything is simply happy.
—OSHO

Beacons of hope are everywhere. They are country church steeples and shiny barn roofs in afternoon light; little soft-serve ice cream stands and groups of people laughing together, free from self-consciousness; an old couple holding hands; traffic as it loosens and flows again after being jammed up; the smell of barbecues and wood smoke; hot bread with soft butter; and a good long hug from someone we love.

These things and others like them are beacons because they remind us of life's soft curves. They are symbols of pleasure, relaxation, contemplation, and love. Seeing them evokes vacation mode, the recollection of spiritual satisfaction, and sensory delight. Any time we stop being so busy and actually take a look around, there are reminders ... everywhere ... of small pleasures and beauty—symbols pointing the way to what life is really all about.

I look around today and see beauty everywhere I look.

June 29

Simplicity is the ultimate sophistication.
—Leonardo da Vinci

Straightforward
Clear
Simple
Near
No need to over-complicate the day

I keep it simple and focus on what is right in front of me.

June 30

In every real man a child is hidden that wants to play.
—FRIEDRICH NIETZSCHE

We suffer from too much seriousness. We are accomplishment-based and stress-based. We overfill the day. We do more, and more yet again. We live on the cusp of burnout.

But life wants us to play and have fun. It wants us to giggle. It wants us to tip like a teapot and spin in a circle and jump for joy. We used to know how to do these things...

And we can learn again! Being playful is an attitude and an approach. It waits patiently. Then, when we invite it out, it smiles hopefully and almost bashfully, unsure. Is it really okay to be silly? Yes! It's good for the soul. Let's sing at the top of our lungs and dance like crazy. Let's howl like a coyote! Let's skip! Let's wobble our tongues and make a tongue-wobbling sound! Let's smile and laugh out loud.

I relax and allow myself to be playful.

July 1

Be careful of your thoughts; they may become words at any moment.
—IRA GASSEN

Names and unkind words have a way of sticking and sinking in. When parents say to their children, "You're bad," "You're clumsy," "You're messy," "You're stupid," the children have a way of absorbing this information like a sponge and storing it as fact. Let's bring ever higher awareness to the way we talk to others, and the way we talk to ourselves. It feels so much better all the way around to focus on the positive. "You're so responsible!" "You're graceful, smart, pretty." "You're so good at organizing things." "You're beautiful and creative." "You have a wonderful sense of humor."

Ahh ... it's a whole different universe that these words and thoughts occupy, and that's the space where I want to hang out. I don't want to contribute to the hurt feelings or the harm of anyone, not with my actions *or* my words. There is enough harm in the world already.

> *I look for the positive in everyone I encounter*
> *and spread compliments instead of judgments.*

July 2

The cyclone derives its power from a calm center. So does a person.
—Norman Vincent Peale

Life has a way of getting busy. It's not unusual to be operating in multiple directions at the same time, and in multiple emotional dimensions as well. When there is a lot going on, it's easy to become speedy energetically, to talk faster and drink a little extra caffeine and be jacked up. But perhaps a better attitude for the business of life is super-calm. It's worth considering. From that space, we can make our decisions from a grounded and thoughtful position.

There's something addictive and exciting about handling multiple situations at once. It's challenging and jazzy—phone calls here, meetings there, business, family, the day's to-do list. This multi-tasking may be thrilling on some level, but it burns us out. For the long haul we need to be strong and steady. It's a mindset. It's a decision not to be drawn off course, and instead to be focused and grounded and smart.

> *I catch myself getting frazzled and stop.*
> *I need to be strong and steady for the long haul.*

July 3

The problem is thinking that having problems is a problem.
—THEODORE RUBIN

Fear is a creeping trickle under the skin. It is panic that is pretending to stay calm. It hooks us at the level of our limiting beliefs—that we are not good enough somehow—and we hang by these hooks.

But everything can be resolved. We think that if our first idea doesn't work then nothing will, but it's not true. We have to remember that for every plan, there is a plan B, and there's no need to be afraid to use it. We don't always get it right the first time, but this fact doesn't make us worthless. It simply means that we're human, and in the process of figuring something out.

I am not bad or wrong if I can't make something work.
It just means I have to keep trying.

July 4

We must be free not because we claim freedom,
but because we practice it.
—WILLIAM FAULKNER

The Fourth of July. It's festive and hot, the height of summer, with barbeques galore. It's parades and fireworks and small children with sparklers. It's a fair amount of patient waiting for things to begin. It's loud and somewhat frantic, a chaotic celebration of freedom and independence. Let's pause for a moment and consider our own personal sense of freedom.

Are we free? Do we *feel* free? Do we *act* free? Or are we oppressed in a self-imposed kind of way by our life circumstances? Are we enslaved by our children, our jobs, our families, or our own negative judgment? Are we martyred? Unappreciated? Do we feel stuck?

Everything is a choice in life. Everything. Let's choose freedom. Let's choose to enjoy the things we do and the people we are. Let's live life with no stress, no strain, no imprisonment, and no warfare. It's up to us to feel free. Freedom is not our right. It's our choice.

I choose freedom.

July 5

You can't run away from trouble. There ain't no place that far.
—UNCLE REMUS

When a life situation gets uncomfortable, my instinct is to bolt. I am an escape artist from way back. There is a certain relief in running, but it's short-lived, and eventually, I always have to face up. We all do.

It's actually easier to stay where we are. If we run every time life gets hard, we will be running forever. But if, on the other hand, we stay and face up, we will discover that we have endless wells within us, of creativity, resilience, courage, and grace.

I am willing to hold my ground and face whatever comes.

July 6

The time to relax is when you don't have time for it.
—SYDNEY J. HARRIS

I am so anxious to check things off my to-do list that I often miss the pleasure of doing them. I put pressure on myself to hurry up so I can move on to the next thing, and the next. I try to maximize my time and squish hours of work into minutes ... all so that I can relax.

While things remain undone, I feel like I have to keep on going, and keep on, until everything is finished and accounted for, and tied with a bow and put away. What insanity! It's *never* all done. On the heels of one project comes another and another. Challenge follows challenge. I want to learn to take my time, enjoy the "doing process," and relax along the way.

I can relax even if I'm in the midst of doing things.

July 7

Criticizing another's garden doesn't keep the weeds out of your own.
—PROVERB

We needn't waste any time criticizing other people. We can rest assured that they are plenty thorough in criticizing themselves. We all know how to ride ourselves mercilessly. We tell ourselves that we should and shouldn't do this, that, and the other thing, and we think negative thoughts about every aspect of our being. It's sad and unnecessary that we do this, but it's true. Let's be positive instead, and look for the good stuff. Let's be forgiving and encouraging. Life feels so much better that way, and it keeps us in the light.

I stop criticizing everything and enjoy my life.

July 8

Envy is the art of counting the other fellow's blessings
instead of your own.
—HAROLD COFFIN

It's an interesting dynamic when we hold ourselves to a certain standard of behavior and then feel irritated when others do not hold themselves to the same. We feel that life is somehow unfair because others don't care about these things the way we do. But how we live is our *choice*, after all, just as it is theirs to do things differently.

Being irritated with others for choosing the "wrong" thing is ridiculous. It changes nothing and makes us miserable. If we want to be happy, we must learn to live and let live, to stop trying to control what other people do or don't do. We must learn to shrug and smile and say, "Oh well. It might not work for me, but it seems to work for her." To be constantly harping and poking and pushing and trying to get others to change the way they *are* in order for us to feel better is useless and angst-producing, and definitely not worth our precious time.

If others have different standards of conduct, that's okay with me.
What I do is my choice, and what they do is theirs.

July 9

Jealousy is the great exaggerator.
—J. C Friedrich von Schiller

Sometimes when we meet people we allow ourselves to be impressed with them in a way that blows reality all out of proportion. We make assumptions based on our own insecurities. We compare ourselves to them and feel inferior. But often, these first impressions do not play out. In further interactions we begin to see that we may have overblown things, and that we were mistaken.

I'd like to not compare myself to others in the first place, and to know that if someone is good at something I'm good at, that person's being good doesn't somehow make me less good. It makes us both good in our own unique ways. I want to celebrate everyone's gifts and life contributions and not feel threatened. I want to know that I am just right as I am, and that there is enough love, enough appreciation, enough respect, and enough recognition to go around. The more there is, the more there is. I am tired of believing in limited supplies.

I trust in the abundant universe
and that there is enough of everything to go around.

A day is Eternity's seed.
—ERIKA HARRIS

Commitment to small changes in life makes a big difference over time. Parking farther away from our destinations so that we have to walk a bit, stopping cursing, making a point to say please and thank you, adding a single stretch to the morning routine and one less cup of coffee—all of these things change the quality of a day's experience.

We all have our habits in life that make us cringe. But we can weed them out. We can recognize when we have picked them up and put them down instead. We can catch ourselves and stop. And if we stop often enough, we will train ourselves not to begin at all. Some behaviors are best made extinct. We need not act on everything we think of. Sometimes silence and non-action are the most powerful and healthy actions there are, and used consistently, in the right way over time, they can help us grow in bounds, like giant oak trees.

> *I recognize when I behave in ways*
> *that make me feel bad, and stop.*

$\mathcal{July}\ 11$

It took me a long time not to judge myself through someone else's eyes.
—SALLY FIELD

It's a challenge to divorce ourselves from what other people think about us. We wonder. We fret. It seems so important. What does this one think? What does that one think? We can't possibly please everybody, but why do we even want to? Why does it matter so much? We want others to think we are all these great things and to approve of our decisions and choices. But the truth is that what they think is a reflection of who *they* are and where they're coming from, and really has nothing at all to do with us.

What power we give to others to determine our worth! Let's take our power back! Let's have the courage to be who we are *without* apology. Let's choose what suits us and not what we think might win the approval of some other. Let's honor *our* truth and live free and confident. Let's release ourselves from the bondage of what others may or may not think about what we do and the way we go about things.

I free myself from the opinions of others.

July 12

The hardest thing to learn in life
is which bridge to cross and which to burn.
—DAVID RUSSELL

How do I know when to stand up when others are thrusting their agendas on me, and when to let it go? It's a question of picking my battles. Where am I willing to commit my forces and risk injury to protect an idea or a principle or my physical safety, and where am I willing to surrender and not fight? Not fighting is often the winning position, but I seem to travel so easily from surrender to doormat. The truth is that I don't want to fight *or* be a doormat. I want to be respected. I want people to not push my boundaries. But that's wanting the world to be what the world is not.

The answer is an inside job. I need to pause when I feel heat from others. I need to breathe and consider and not get all hooked in and explosive. If something is asked of me and I am not sure, I will say so, and express my need for time. Then I can come back to it thoughtfully and be in accordance with my whole self, and be clear about where I stand on the issue, and why.

I take the time to know where I stand
on all issues and set my boundaries accordingly.

July 13

The man who never alters his opinion
is like standing water, and breeds reptiles of the mind.
—WILLIAM BLAKE

What pleases me today may not please me next week. Sometimes I become consumed with a song and listen to it over and over, and then a month or so later when it comes on I will change the station because I'm sick of it. What is earth-shattering today is no big deal next week.

I believe the point of my life is to grow and change and evolve, so anything that is static and unchanging does not serve life's purpose. I may think I want some sort of perfect predictable stability, but I don't really. What I want is experience and challenge and all the rising emotions that bubble up and recede to teach me, and then remind me, and then to teach me again, that nothing is absolute and that everything comes and goes. The more comfortable I am with the changeability and inconstancy of life, the more peace I will experience.

I accept the variability of life.

July 14

The body is your temple. Keep it pure and clean.
—B.K.S. IYENGAR

We seem to think we're never good enough physically. We are either too tall or too short, or too fat or too thin, or too muscular or not muscular enough, or we don't like our arms or hips or chest or chin. It's a rare person who doesn't have something physically that causes them a sense of frustration and unhappiness. Maybe it's achy knees or a tight neck, or a nose that is too big or earlobes that are too long. We abuse our bodies with negative thinking.

Let's change our approach. Let's appreciate our bodies for all they do for us, for their functionality and strength and the curves of our bones and muscles. Let's be grateful for our hands and fingers, our skin and eyes and back, for our thighs and belly, and our very breath! Thank you, body, for standing by me all these years, even when I have not stood by you.

I appreciate my body!

$\mathcal{July}$ 15

All changes, even the most longed for, have their melancholy;
for what we leave behind us is a part of ourselves;
we must die to one life before we can enter another.
—ANATOLE FRANCE

When faced with something new and unfamiliar, it's natural to be suspicious and feel a certain sense of fear and even dislike. Something new—a new routine, a new arrangement of furniture, a new way of doing things—can't possibly be as comfortable as the old way. The old way is familiar and well-worn, well-known.

The unknown is scary, but we don't have to feel afraid. We can be open to it and welcome it as it is. We get to know it slowly and find our way. It doesn't take long for it to become familiar. We learn to love its gifts and accept its limitations. Through the process of adaptation and familiarity, we learn to trust what is new and unknown, and then it is no longer new. Then it is the "new" old and faithful.

I face the "new" in my life with courage and faith.
I trust in its purpose in my life.

July 16

How simple it is to see that we can only be happy now.
—GERALD JAMPOLSKY

I can get so caught up in future possibilities for happiness that I miss the small pleasures of the day. Small pleasures abound. Each experience has its own rich world of sensation: the dark morning, cold water on my face, the taste of breakfast, and the emerging light and unfolding of the day. If I don't enjoy these small pleasures, and all the others like them, I miss out on life's bounty. I get lost in thoughts of the past and future.

Let's be aware of our traveling minds and commit to bringing them back to the present moment and the experience of each thing. Let's commit to bringing them back, and bringing them back again. As many times as our minds travel, let's bring them back to the present.

> *I am mindful and present. I enjoy the day and all of*
> *its experiences. I am grateful for the unexpected*
> *blessings of life's small pleasures.*

July 17

Don't handicap your children by making their lives easy.
—ROBERT A. HEINLEIN

Our wanting to "fix" our children does not mean they are necessarily broken. They are who they are, and have come here to learn lessons, to age gracefully or to die young, to be wildly successful or sick and addictive, or both, or a little bit of everything. Letting go of our children in healthy ways is no easy business. Because we feel they belong to us in some way, it seems our job to change them, help them, mold them, encourage them, and do all that we can to ensure that they suffer as little as possible.

But even with all of our desire and effort and good intentions, our children go their own way, and feel how they feel, and do what they do. Perhaps our real job as parents is not to mold our children as we think they should be, but to unconditionally accept them as they are, and love them for all of their faults and struggles as well as their gifts.

*I back off and allow my children the space they need
to figure out their own lives. I love them no matter what.*

July 18

Faith is believing that the outcome will be what it should be,
no matter what it is.
—COLETTE BARON-REID

I don't understand how things always seem to work out, but they do. What is needed is provided. What seems impossible to overcome is overcome. Fear is faced. Loss is grieved. Darkness becomes blessing, and hope really does spring eternal. Perhaps it's fortitude and courage and human ingenuity that get us through, but more likely it's the grace of God.

Solutions to problems come entirely out of nowhere. My little fantasy plans and designs are utterly swamped by miraculous serendipity. Trying to "figure things out" is overrated. I don't have to micro-manage and control all the people and details of my life. I can watch with patience and curiosity. I can accept the gifts of the unpredictable, live in the air and space of all possibility, and remember that things always seem to have a way of working out against all odds.

I welcome the future with curiosity
and trust in unexpected goodness.

July 19

*Do life's plain, common work as it comes, certain that daily duties
and daily bread are the sweetest things in life.*
—Robert Louis Stevenson

I love my routines. I look forward to the predictability of the order in which I choose to do things, and the process I have developed over time for the inclusion of all of my daily duties. Routines stabilize and ground me. And whenever something new comes along, it doesn't take long to create routines around the newness, to accommodate it and hold it down in my world like tent stakes. When there is no structure, I create one like scaffolding, a place to hang my security and steady my boots.

My gratitude today is for routines and for sensible ways of getting things done, for the comfort of repetition, the easy accommodation of ever-changing demands, and the supportive structure of daily maintenance.

I appreciate and enjoy the routines of my life.

July 20

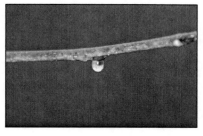

Life is short, but there is always time for courtesy.
—RALPH WALDO EMERSON

It's a worthwhile practice to leave things better than we found them, and maybe to leave people better than we found them as well. Our presence can be a drain on others and on the environment, or it can be like a gentle soaking rain, full of blessings and relief. It's easy to be hard on things, to break them and make a mess, to be careless and haphazard with the way we use them, to leave them lying around or not properly cleaned after use. And it's easy to be hard on people in somewhat the same way. It takes attention to be thoughtful and to care, but it's most definitely worth our time and effort.

> *I leave every aspect of the environment I occupy today better than when I found it.*

July 21

Genius is nothing but a great aptitude for patience.
—GEORGES-LOUIS LECLERC DE BUFFON

Most things that happen in my life do not happen according to my time frame. They happen when they happen, and I scramble to keep up, or else wait, and wait, trying to maintain my enthusiasm and faith. Understanding this concept, I am learning to stop making such vigorous plans. If a situation forces deviation from my agenda, I can roll with it. I don't need to impose my schedule on life. I can shrug and be flexible. I can smile and say okay to the changes in my visionary timeline. I can be open-minded enough to entertain the possibility that things *could* work out even better with the new plan. Maybe it's an upgrade. Maybe it's a blessing in disguise. That's what I am going to choose to believe.

*I free my future from the imposition of a planned-out timeline
and all the things I think I want to see unfold.
I trust in the happenings of my life.*

*I make a bonfire of all sorrows... I blaze my way through
the darkness of all minds.*
—PARAMAHANSA YOGANANDA

The ability to pick oneself up by the bootstraps, to cultivate drive and purpose deep within and express it in productive ways externally, is an art form no less than sculpture or painting. We all have this deep inner power. It's the creative fountain, the idea when all ideas have run out, and the enthusiasm beyond exhaustion.

Let's dig deep today and wake up to our power. Let's recognize that we carry our motivation within us, and that we can breathe it up at any time. We can accomplish great things. We can face what comes with assurance, knowing that we have a fire inside of us that is limitless. It's ours to ignore or explore as we choose.

I breathe deeply and draw upon my inner power.

July 23

For fast acting relief, try slowing down.
—LILY TOMLIN

Being partway through a process frustrates me on some level. I like to gulp my problems like a dog gulps his dinner. I want to get to the bottom of the bowl. But when one issue is resolved, immediately on its tail comes the next one, and the next.

I want to find a way to relax throughout the process. I want to lose my urgent need to get it all done right now, right this minute. I want to enjoy my efforts while they happen instead of looking at some distant point on the horizon and believing that there, at that special place in the future, when all the work is done, I will be whole and happy and completely fulfilled, and I can relax at last. The only trouble is, when the work is done, so is the journey. The journey *is* the work. When it's over, so am I.

I slow down today and remember to savor my life.

July 24

The body never lies.
—MARTHA GRAHAM

I believe in therapeutic movement for each body, each imbalance, each structural deficiency, and each injury. I trust the body. I trust that it knows just what it needs, and speaks to us if we will only listen. I believe it has an innate ability and drive to heal itself, and that it will continue on vibrantly for a long time in spite of our neglecting and abusing it, but that ultimately it cannot thrive without care and appreciation. And that includes the way we think about it, and our level of trust in its strength and stamina.

Constantly mollycoddling our daily physical conditions and overblowing them makes for a body much like an overprotected child. Let's allow our bodies to romp and be playful and find their movement. Let's not limit them with fear in our minds, or else they will be small and lack courage. Let's work with our bodies to achieve great vitality and great energy and strength beyond our wildest dreams.

> *I treat my body with appreciation and respect.*
> *I pay attention to what it has to tell me.*

$$\mathcal{J}uly\ 25$$

Obsession is the single most wasteful human activity.
—NORMAN MAILER

Obsession with anything creates a problem in our lives because it weights us too heavily to one psychological spot. Obsession with being too healthy makes us unhealthy in a way. Obsession with being thin and body-perfect leads to feelings of inadequacy. Obsession in intimate relationships generates clinginess and need in one partner and feelings of suffocation in the other. Obsession with being in control leaves us angry and bitter, because there is so much that we can't control, no matter how hard we push.

There's no payoff for obsession that makes it worth it. Being consumed with one thing or another to the exclusion of all else makes us old before our time. It's an out-of-whack way to live, with no balance and no internal peace. We don't need to wear life like a straitjacket. Most of us have been wrapped too tight for long enough.

I let go of my obsessions and live free in the present moment.

July 26

I have never found a companion that was so companionable as solitude.
—HENRY DAVID THOREAU

Every so often I get worn down by too many things going on in my life and all of the things I feel I have to do. I'm burned out and dried up, and it's my responsibility to recognize that and take the necessary steps to replenish my spirit. The challenge for me is taking the time I need without guilt, when there is work to be done and there are things to accomplish, when anyone I love might be struggling and need me to be there. But I can't help with a dried-up spirit, not really. I can only drive myself further into depletion, and then I'm no good to anyone.

So it's okay to take my time. It's okay to need solitude and relish it. It's okay to love people, and it's okay to need time and space away from them. If I honor my need, then I come back refreshed and rejuvenated, and we are all better for it.

I take the time I need, when I need it, for my soul's restoration.
I take it without guilt and without apology.

July 27

The door to safety swings on the hinges of common sense.
—AUTHOR UNKNOWN

It takes two reasonable people to reach reasonable conclusions. But there is a whole other category of people in the world with whom no reasoning is possible. They are driven by internal demons so deep and convoluted that reality as the rest of us experience it is warped for them, and we are the ones who seem unreasonable to them. And it is not their fault that they are sick, but their behavior takes its toll nonetheless, whether they mean for it to or not.

I used to believe that I could heal these people with my love, but when I have tried, instead of healing them, I have become sick myself. Some who are sick may be healed, but it is certainly not for me to dictate who will be healed or how. That is God's territory. It's my job to recognize who I'm dealing with, to establish healthy boundaries, and to protect myself from danger.

> *I set boundaries with unreasonable people,*
> *and remain vigilant and on guard.*

Getting and spending, we lay waste our powers.
—WILLIAM WORDSWORTH

We never even put our hands on most of the money that we make and spend. It's all representative, the moving of numbers on a page from one place to the next. And this whole system has enormous power to upset our equilibrium and potentially fill us with more fear on a daily basis than anything else in our lives, except perhaps the fear of death.

But it's all fantasy! Our worth is no more determined by the balance of our bank account than by the opinions of other people. Our quality is in our character. We can be poor and noble. We can live a simple and clean life with very little income. We can be kind and express love even if we don't have fancy cars or huge savings accounts. And the reverse is true as well. We can be rich and noble, or rich and miserable. It is really not money that determines the quality of our lives at all, but the quality of our lives that determines the worth of our money.

I can be happy and healthy
no matter how much money I have, or don't have.

July 29

A handful of patience is worth more than a bushel of brains.
—DUTCH PROVERB

We can wait impatiently, with irritation and tension filling our every nerve, or we can wait with curiosity. We can wait nervously or without any sense of urgency whatsoever. When we are unhappy while we wait, it's because we don't want to be where we are. We are resisting what is. It's the resistance that creates our tension, not the waiting itself.

It's not the situation that's the problem. It's our not liking it. It's our wanting it to be other than it is. If we calm down, there is a certain peace always available to us, and it comes from inside. Whatever we are stuck in may not be what we would choose, but for whatever reason it has chosen us. We can resist it and be miserable, or we can go with the flow and trust that whatever it is will be exactly what it's supposed to be.

I choose a patient, playful attitude for the day's situations.

July 30

A smile is a curve that sets everything straight.
—PHYLLIS DILLER

Every behavior has a pull to it. If someone is feeling down and dark and encounters someone who is up and full of light, usually one of two things happens. The down individual is lifted up, or the up individual is brought down. It depends on which energy has the stronger pull. Generally speaking, if we are miserable, we will bring out the miserable in others, and if we want happiness, we need to be happy.

Let's be aware of what we are sending out emotionally, as well as what's coming our way. We don't have to respond to selfishness by being selfish, or become irritated if the person we are dealing with is behaving that way. We can face life with a smile. We can respond to most things with love and kindness, in spite of whatever darkness may be exerting its pull.

I will be what I want to experience.

July 31

Curiosity is a willing, a proud, an eager confession of ignorance.
—S. LEONARD RUBINSTEIN

Everything in my life seems to unfold as a face-off and a confrontation at first, and then a struggle, and finally, a settling in. I'd like to spare myself the initial fighting if at all possible, perhaps by approaching new things with curiosity instead of a desire to conquer. Curiosity feels gentle and friendly—a quiet exploration instead of a challenge and a compulsion to take down. I prefer the energy of curiosity. At least, I prefer the *idea* of it. I invite curiosity into my life. I welcome it fully. I am willing to pause and look instead of jumping in with both feet. I am willing to consider options and possibilities beyond my instinctual first blast of attack.

Let me be curious today, and thoughtful.
Let me be free from all battling confrontation, with people,
with projects, and with anything new that I may face.

August 1

If you want to turn your life around, try thankfulness.
—GERALD GOOD

I have heard people say, and really believe, that they have nothing to be grateful for, which is nonsense. Let's begin with the basics. We have functioning bodies that move us around. We have intelligence and creativity. We have hope and possibility and a world full of natural beauty. We have clothes and food and cars and houses. We have life and a heart and dreams. We have the ability to love and be loved. We are each of us blessed beyond measure, if we can only see it, every moment of every day.

I am grateful today. I know that I am deeply blessed.

August 2

Habits are at first cobwebs, then cables.
—SPANISH PROVERB

If I do something beneficial once in a blue moon, I am unlikely to experience any particular positive result. If I perform the same activity weekly, I might get a sense of limited progress. Twice a week would produce more noticeable results, and three times a week even more so. And if I were to do the same beneficial action every day, or even five times a week, for a year, my life could change profoundly.

We tend to dabble and play around. We try something, feel better, and then promptly stop. Or we look to others to motivate us, and if the other isn't there, we fall off course and lack the self-motivation to continue. But when we are steady and consistent, when we make it a habit to do the things that make us feel good, then we feel good! Imagine that. We can experience positive results in our lives if we are willing to do a little bit of daily work. Let's step up. We're worth the effort.

> *I commit to positive daily habits*
> *so that I might experience positive daily results.*

August 3

For such loss, I would believe, abundant recompense.
—WILLIAM WORDSWORTH

The worst kind of betrayal is the one where we betray our own value system, where we use our logic to justify something that we know in our heart is wrong. Even if no one catches us, we have to live with our own feeling of internal seediness. It's an error to think that we can get away with something. One way or another, the dues for our choices always have to be paid.

It happens to us all sooner or later. Our innocence is lost. The price tag is pain and suffering, but as with all things, there is reward as well. There is wisdom and more peaceful living if we can learn from our mistakes. We can learn to choose better. We can feel satisfaction in our decisions and pride in our integrity. We can honor our values and the lives we live, and we needn't ever betray ourselves again.

> *I pay attention to my moral compass*
> *and live in integrity with myself.*

Children have more need of models than of critics.
—CAROLYN COATS

At times, I have discovered in myself a tendency to speak to my children in ways that I would never speak to anyone else. I make demands. I tell them what they are going to do and how it's going to be, and when I do this, they bristle and resist me, and we find ourselves in stand-off mode.

This shows a lack of respect on my part. Instead of asking for their input or asking their permission, I discount their feelings and make some absolute statement about my expectations. That may fly when they are age five or even nine, but it no longer has an appropriate application when they are seventeen. I give them adult responsibilities, but I still want to treat them as children, and they are willing to accept that role when it's convenient. But they can't have it both ways, and neither can I. It's time to leave the shores of childhood behind. They need to grow up, and so do I.

I treat my children with courtesy and respect.

As soon as you stop wanting something, you get it.
—ANDY WARHOL

The other day I witnessed a young girl having an emotional breakdown over wanting something that her mother would not let her have. Her face was red and blotchy. She kept repeating over and over through her desperate, gasping sobs, "But I really want it, Mommy. I *really* want it." As if that should be enough. As if her wanting it badly enough, and expressing her desire tirelessly enough, must surely guarantee her success in getting it. And if we're honest, don't we all get that way? We may not sob and beg, but internally we are whining and moaning no less than the little girl.

And yet, we often want things and even succeed in getting things that turn out to be bad for us and bring us nothing but grief. Life goes better when we stop demanding that it be a certain way and enjoy it for being whatever it is. Each day holds its perfect mix of things we want and things we need. It only fails us if we have something else in mind.

> *I want what I have. I refrain from childish tantrums*
> *and internal whining.*

August 6

Faith makes the discords of the present the harmonies of the future.
—ROBERT COLLYER

What seems like the end of everything can actually turn out to be a beginning instead, and a blessing in disguise. But even knowing this, my faith falters. I have a tendency to want to avoid suffering at all costs, for myself as well as the people I love. And yet, so much of my own growth in life has come through difficulties and hardship. I have learned through experience that bad things are not necessarily bad, and appearances can deceive me.

It's not my job to know what's what in every situation, but only to trust in something bigger than me. I can surrender to believing in goodness and thinking that all is well in the grand scheme of things, or I can be a victim and survive miserably, jockeying for position and going forever to catastrophe in my head.

I choose faith over fear today, and say no to catastrophic thinking.

August 7

*When dealing with people, remember you are not dealing
with creatures of logic, but creatures of emotion.*
—DALE CARNEGIE

We can feel two things at once: excitement and dread, fear and
hope, love and hostility, courage and trepidation. Paradox seems as
much a part of life as the changeability of the weather. It's a little
of this and a little of that. And I am the same way. I am enormous
and tiny. I can't wait and I'm terrified to begin. I just ate and I'm
still hungry.

The multiplicity of emotion is like the pepper of life, the spice
rack of our daily fare. So I'll take it, and enjoy the variety of each
day's flavor. I have some peace and a bit of anxiety, vibrant energy
and bone-tired exhaustion, tenderness and explosive strength. I
have joy and calm and stress and frustration. I have happiness and
fear. I have all of life's grand emotions and the blessing each day to
be able to feel them all.

I welcome the experience of my emotions today.
I witness their variety, and the rise and fall of each one.
I am grateful to be alive and to feel the range of feelings that I feel.

August 8

Labels are for clothing. Labels are not for people.
—MARTINA NAVRATILOVA

We like identifying labels, and use them frequently. He's shy, and she's pretty but insensitive, and that guy over there is a hypochondriac. And with all of the labels that we slap on everyone else, it may be instructive to consider how we might be labeling ourselves.

Let's bring awareness to the limitations of our labels. Let's avoid the use of words like "always" and "never," and judgments that close doors on the possibility of change. Let's cut the world a break and allow for the possibility that we don't ever know the whole story, even with ourselves. How we behave and the ailments we suffer from are circumstances of our lives, but they are not who we are. We can have issues and struggles, but we need not *be* them. We are bigger and greater and full of more variation and changeability than any label can possibly describe.

> *I refrain from using labels. I allow for possibility*
> *and accept that I have a limited view.*

August 9

A vacation is like love: anticipated with pleasure,
experienced with discomfort, and remembered with nostalgia.
—AUTHOR UNKNOWN

Vacations are hard work. We plan them and rearrange our lives. Then we pack and travel. Once arrived and settled, we adjust the best we can to unfamiliar beds and pillows and the reality of our experience as it stands up against our expectations. The weather, traffic, sickness, the wrong clothes, the attitudes of our traveling companions—all of these things are wild cards.

And then, when it's all over, we have to travel home … and unpack, and do loads of laundry, and regroup. We have to return to our lives, and work, and the next thing, and the next, with our trip now behind us. And no matter what kind of time we had, it becomes nostalgic. The adventure becomes a "classic" in our lives, even if it was nothing but hardship. And we smile every time we remember it … just knowing that we made it through.

I live my life like I live my vacations: with a willingness to
experience whatever comes, knowing that whatever happens,
or doesn't happen, it will help me grow in the end.

August 10

*I would advise all aspiring youths aspiring to athletic fame
or a professional career to practice clean living, fair play,
and good sportsmanship.*
—Major Taylor

When we are needy, it's a turn-off. People are more inclined to give to those who are doing the best they can without complaint. There's something about whining and self-pity that seems to ask for punishment instead of reward.

Perhaps we could all use a bit more of a chin-up kind of attitude when faced with challenges. Good sportsmanship in life, as in sports, is appreciated by others, and feels good on the inside, too.

***I bring my best to every experience. I think about what I can
contribute instead of all the things I want to get.***

August 11

Everyone is the age of their heart.
—GUATEMALAN PROVERB

Age is a state of mind as much as it is a state of the body. I know six-year-olds who are like old women, and old women who are like little girls. The adult-like children are serious and well behaved. They are scornful of laughter and silliness, which is something that the childlike adults embrace. I'm not sure where or how we learn that growing older in years has to mean loss of mobility and spontaneity. Whose rule is that?

Let's not be old before our time. Let's not become musty and inflexible in our thinking or our actions. Let's move and stretch and dance. Let's walk and read and enjoy life's simple pleasures, unafraid of getting "old." Let's lovingly accept our changing bodies and become ever-better caretakers of ourselves. Let's remember the importance of play and have fun with our time. Let's celebrate life every day that we live.

> *I enjoy my vitality today.*
> *I am playful and curious and bright and alive.*

August 12

*Everyone is kneaded out of the same dough
but not baked in the same oven.*
—YIDDISH PROVERB

We are each on an individual journey, but we travel together down the human path. It takes the company of another to point things out to us that we cannot see. It's a give-and-take process, a sharing adventure. It's unhealthy and uncomfortable to live in isolation. Solitude is one thing, but the complete avoidance of human interaction robs us of the richness of living fully. We need each other. We need each other for comfort and understanding and lessons and solutions, for insight and inspiration, for encouragement and love. We need each other for conversation, to test our limits and set boundaries, and to realize how we are separate and how we are forever the same. Let's reach out today. Let's enrich our lives with a fresh perspective.

> *I am a grateful member of the human race.*
> *I give and take. I share my perspective and am open*
> *to the perspective of others.*

August 13

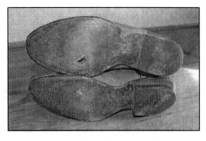

You have brains in your head. You have feet in your shoes.
You can steer yourself any direction you choose.
—Dr. Seuss

I have never understood the excitement over a pair of new shoes. I prefer old shoes, and always have. New shoes are too clean, too stiff, and too slippery on the soles. They are awkward. They rub in strange places. They call out their newness in every way. Old shoes are comfortable and inviting. They welcome the curves of my heels and toes. But the trouble is that much as I love them and wear them, I wear them out, so new shoes have to be acquired. They are a necessity.

And life can be just like shoes. It can be comfortably worn-in, or it can be worn-out. Life can be brand-new and slippery, or it can have holes in the toes and be paper-thin. We need newness on occasion, and when we do, the only thing to do is to feel the pinch until it stretches out, to wear the new until we wear it in.

I accept the stiffness and the pinching of new life and new shoes.
They both become comfortable in time.

August 14

Precisely the least, the softest, lightest, a lizard's rustling, a breath,
a flash, a moment—a little makes the way of the best happiness.
—FRIEDRICH NIETZSCHE

I cannot plan for the most powerful, moving, and beautiful moments of my life. I just have to show up for them. Anticipating some great event, I have fantasy visions of how I will be touched and inspired by certain happenings, but in the end, I am blessed with what I cannot foresee. I try to guarantee magic by planning the details. But the magic comes in spite of me, and from unexpected distances, and sideways. It comes from the least likely sources. It whispers or comes banging and rattling. It makes itself known by speeding up my heartbeat and overwhelming me with tears, laughter, and tingling skin. It makes itself known by all of these together or one at a time, by the power surge of love and gratitude and the sheer inexplicable beauty of fragile humanity. It makes itself known by all of the unexpected things that move me to the experience of absolute joy.

> *I show up for life. I open to my blessings and stop*
> *trying to manipulate the future.*

August 15

Organization is everything.
—GRUFF HERRMAN

It's hard for me to feel at ease when there are discombobulating elements in my life: decisions hanging in the balance, paperwork in disarray, or a too-long list of duties undone. I accept that loose ends are part of my journey, and that I don't ever get to a point of "arrival" where everything is exactly how and where I want it to be. But still, things in my world require mental and physical organization on a regular basis.

I am most comfortable when everything is in its proper place in the file cabinet of my mind. I have files for things to get done that simply require my time, and I have files for next-step action on lifelong projects. There are life's daily chores, and messes that need straightening up immediately before they fester and mold. I cannot skimp on any of it, or I pay the price. I must regularly organize my life at every level. If I do not, I suffer from irritability and a foul temper, and the constant noise and rattling of a fretful and overwhelmed mind.

I take care of all of the little things that are causing me irritation.

August 16

Everything should be made as simple as possible, but not simpler.
—ALBERT EINSTEIN

The simplest ideas are often the best ones. Our high-tech, high-speed world is complicated and overwhelming. What is basic and repetitive soothes our scattered souls.

We have a tendency to think that fancy is better, and that the more complex something is, the more important it must be. But maybe not. Maybe the basics are the ticket and the key to real happiness. Maybe what's simplest is what's most profound, and maybe what's most accessible is the very thing that we are seeking … only it is so close that we cannot see it.

I stick to what matters and let go of the rest.
I keep my life simple and feel good.

August 17

The windows of my soul I throw
Wide open to the sun.
—John Greenleaf Whittier

I am happily aware of the changing seasonal light and the morning chill of the coming fall. I feel a loss and sadness for the summer passing away yet again, but autumn brings its own kind of blessing. It feels like renewal to me, and absolute freshness. It is crisp and breezy and full of delicious smells and beautiful colors. It fills me with hope and possibility, maybe even more so than the spring. While the spring is full of purpose and work in the garden and lawn cutting, the fall is easy and gentle and settling in. It's slowing down and spiritual restoration. I welcome it gladly. I enjoy the changing slant of the sun and the elongated shadows.

But it's not here yet, not fully. Fall is coming, but is not quite here, and the summer is ending, but has not quite ended. I want to enjoy this transitional time. I want to enjoy the summer that remains and the touches of stretching fall light that signify what's to come.

I am constantly in flux, like the seasons,
and I enjoy the beauty of the ever-changing light.

233

August 18

Man embraces in his makeup all the natural orders;
he's a squid, a mollusk, a sucker and a buzzard.
—MARTIN H. FISCHER

Strip away the jewelry and haircuts and fancy clothes! Strip away the bank accounts and expensive cars! Strip away the divisions of class and culture and all the levels of education! No matter who we are or where we come from, we are all the same. We put on our clothes and waltz through our days pretending that we are above the lowness of digestion and elimination, but we are not. Our bodily functions equalize us. We get hurt. We get sick. And we all bleed red when we get sliced open.

I accept that I am fully human, and no better or less than any other human, so I have compassion, and I keep an open mind.

Enjoyment comes fleetingly and unheralded;
I cannot determinedly enjoy myself.
—ROBERTSON DAVIES

Sometimes I take time off, and it's my time to fill as I please. But rather than seeking relaxation, I always seem to pack my free time with too many activities and end up feeling pressure going from one thing to the next, and feeling panicky as my time runs out. And so, instead of being pleasing, my pursuit of pleasure ends up being stressful. I think we do the same thing with weekends and vacations and anything that is supposed to be "fun." We overplan and over-obligate and overload, and end up exhausted instead of refreshed.

Let's remember the sense of tension we feel when we overfill our time off. If we don't relax, we defeat the purpose, and possibly end up even more stressed-out than we were before, instead of feeling rejuvenated and restored. Rejuvenation is what we need.

I keep my free time free, and allow my recovery time
from work to help me recover.

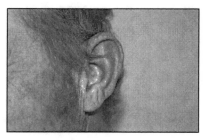

The most precious gift we can offer anyone is our attention.
—Thich Nhat Hanh

We hear what we want to hear, no matter what is being said. Often we do not even wait for a person to stop talking before we begin our response, because we know in advance what our response is going to be to what we are sure they are saying. How arrogant of us to be so sure we know so much! And yet, we all do it.

Let's commit to listening. That's what we all really want anyway, and need. We long for others to really listen to us with interest and their complete attention. And in return, we can listen to others with *our* full attention. Let's try it! Let's catch ourselves wanting to interrupt and then stop. Let's become silent within ourselves, and curious, and learn to listen from the heart.

I really listen to others today.
I listen with curiosity and compassion and an open heart.

Photography deals exquisitely with appearances,
but nothing is what it appears to be.
—DUANE MICHALS

Sometimes photographs capture a moment, and sometimes they do not. Live action is so full of emotion and perception and temperature and subtle movement and the language of our eyes. The best photographs evoke these many dimensions of life, but most miss the mark entirely. We look forward to seeing pictures of some delightful event, and we're sure the camera will show our beauty and our feelings of ripe joy ... and then it does not. We feel confused and disappointed.

The ultimate lesson is one of letting go. Sometimes we look beautiful in a photograph, and sometimes we don't. What's important to remember is that the purest memory we have of any event we carry not in our photo albums, but in our hearts.

I don't get too hung up on appearances.
What matters most is what I experience on the inside.

August 22

Fear makes the wolf bigger than he is.
—GERMAN PROVERB

There's a difference between being cautious and being tentative. One implies wisdom, and the other, fear. To approach life and risky situations with a certain amount of care, and slow movement, and with our eyes wide open, is one thing. But to hold back because we are afraid we will get hurt is another thing entirely. Caution is a safer bet in the long run. When we are tentative, we are halting and stammering, and in some ways we actually increase our risk. Our hesitation interrupts life flow and creates a jam-up of energy and an opportunity for injury. We are actually disabled by our fears.

Let's move through the day with care and intelligence. And if we find ourselves sticking and hesitating, let's acknowledge the fear we feel but move forward anyway. Let's trust the day and our full range of experience, and not miss out on anything by holding ourselves back.

I am careful but not afraid.

The part can never be well unless the whole is well.
—PLATO

We suffer from our emotional discomfort no less than we suffer from a stiff neck. We get angry and point fingers. We blame others for our suffering. We blame our pillows and our beds. They are contributing factors, but not, I think, the ultimate cause. We must take responsibility for the way we find ourselves on any given day. We are the source of both our injury and our healing.

We have pushed ourselves too hard, or become consumed with catastrophic thinking, or simply fallen asleep in a position that has wrenched us. Resisting whatever the facts are only increases the discomfort. Let's accept where we are today. If we are in pain, let's acknowledge it and treat it with kindness and compassion. Let's not feel irritated or vengeful. Let's accept that it will pass and do the best we can to allow it to be here for as long as it stays.

I accept where I am today. I do not struggle against what is.
If I am in pain, I experience the pain. I have love
and compassion for myself, and I trust the process of my life.

August 24

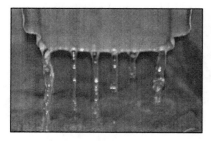

The living moment is everything.
—D. H. LAWRENCE

Being in a relaxed state has never been my strong suit. I do well while engaged in physical activity. I am efficient and productive. I take pleasure in my work. But I want to relax. I have always wanted to be able to relax. I want to let worry and hardship run off me like dripping rain, but I can't force it. I have to let relaxation come, and welcome it when it arrives. I make judgments about what *should* be relaxing to me, and then when it isn't, I feel more stressed than ever, and frustrated.

I am most relaxed when I am fully engaged in being right where I am, wherever that may be, and when I have a sense of gratitude and complete aliveness. I am savoring what is and not rushing to get to something else or mentally straining in any way. That's relaxing! That, for me, is pleasure and rejuvenation and relief.

*I relax into the rhythm of my day. So long as I do not struggle
or strain, I can feel at ease no matter what I am doing.
It's okay to like what I like and to be who I am.*

August 25

Truth will out.
—WILLIAM SHAKESPEARE

I create a lot of unnecessary hardship in my life by trying to convince myself that I can be okay with something I am fundamentally not okay with, and that I can alter the way I think about it by sheer force of will. If only I were a more evolved person, surely I could find a way to be okay with almost anything. But try as I might, the result is not what I hope for. My body acts out what my mind will not acknowledge.

If something does not sit comfortably within me, I may be uncomfortable with it for a very good reason, and I have to be honest about the discomfort I feel. I need to own it. I need to honor my truth. I cannot run away from it, and I cannot turn a blind eye. I have to listen to the voices of my soul and the whisperings of my body. They are there for a reason.

I honor my truth.

Sometimes I think and other times I am.
—PAUL VALÉRY

I can play out an entire drama in my head. I create a plot and stage the first act. How would I react if such and such happened? How would I feel? How would others in the play react? What would it mean? And then I go deeper still: act two. I build resentments. I suffer. Others suffer. In subtle pockets of idle mind time, the plot in my head thickens and develops. My body reacts to the storyline as if it were real. I get a headache and feel tension. A cold starts to come on. And when the mental noise becomes loud enough, I suddenly realize what has happened. This is the beginning of act three: resolution.

And then I have to laugh at myself, because I feel as if I've been through something big, but nothing has actually happened! I'm sure I'm not alone in creating this kind of internal drama, and I'm sure it has its purpose, but what insanity! It's a good reminder to keep my sense of humor and not to take myself too seriously.

I don't get so caught up inside my head that I forget what's actually happening in front of me. The hooks of my thinking will hang me if I let them.

August 27

Things that were hard to bear are sweet to remember.
—SENECA

Sometimes I find the very experience of living to be sad, but in a sweet and beautiful kind of way. There is so much hurt and misunderstanding and judgment and carelessness, all in the same mix as nobility and grace. As humans, we can be so reckless and clumsy, and yet we are capable of the highest acts of kindness and such big love. It's the juxtaposition of the two that I find sad and beautiful all at once.

If we tune in to it, there is a shadow of pain in each of us, even in our happiest moments—the scars of past wrongdoings, the disappointments, our wounds. And the earth feels that way to me also, scathing and polluted with human mistakes and abandoned dreams. But there is beauty in our errors and our imperfections, too. There is the echo of human limitations reverberating over the earth like a bass guitar or a frame drum. And it is not horrible or scary, but rhythmic and humming, comforting almost, and sweet, in a sad sort of way.

There is enough hurt and suffering on earth
without my adding to it. I commit to do no harm.

August 28

To forgive is to set a prisoner free and discover that the prisoner was you.
—LEWIS B. SMEDES

Sometimes we have to forgive others just for being who they are, and forgive ourselves the same. Our journey is ripe with opportunities for ill-timed responses and bad ideas, for unintentional rudeness and overstepping our bounds. And it's all okay, so long as our intentions are good, and even if they aren't. Forgiveness is the best survival tactic I know of. It fills us with compassion and wipes the slate clean of resentment. It gives us a fresh start. We are deserving of it, and so are those with whom we live and work. We are all emotional and reactive. We are all capable of making a mess. We have all been selfish, unkind, judgmental, and afraid. We have all been wrong about something or someone, over and over and over. Why should we expect anyone else to be less so?

I forgive myself for my limitations and imperfections,
and I forgive the limitations and imperfections of all those
I encounter. I am willing to live and let live.

August 29

Know, first, who you are, and then adorn yourself accordingly.
—EPICTETUS

Little girls think nothing of flaunting a pink tutu, or a fancy dress with petticoats, or a princess costume with feathered slippers, out into the world. They wear these things and enjoy the attention they get, and feel beautiful and not at all self-conscious. We become self-conscious as we age. We learn to want to be dressed appropriately. We want to look thin. We become critical of what we wear and how it fits us. As adults, even if we find something that makes us feel beautiful or particularly handsome, we are always a bit unsure. It is not enough that we love it ourselves. We care what other people think, and it has to pass their test, too.

Let's take a lesson from little girls. Let's adorn ourselves in the way that pleases us most. Let's decorate our bodies with delight. Let's *feel* our beauty. Let's know it. Let's *be* it! Beauty, it seems to me, is how we wear ourselves more than what we look like. Let's wear ourselves with confidence. Let's drop our self-consciousness and dress ourselves with joy!

> *I feel the beauty of being who I am, exactly as I am—*
> *imperfect physically, but perfectly me!*

Eliminate the unnecessary so that the necessary may speak.
—HANS HOFMANN

When I am overwhelmed with things to do, what helps me the most is a plan. I take a few minutes to list everything on a piece of paper and look at it. Some things on the list I simply do not have to get done right now, and I cross them off. My priority is for right now. I resolve to let go of perfectionism and accept in advance that I can only do what I can do and no more. I'm not expecting miracles. Contrary to what many of us believe, we don't always have to do our *very best* work… sometimes we just have to do the work, period. I start on the most urgent "have-to" and set a reasonable stop time. I commit to stop even if I'm not finished, and move on to the next thing. A little bit of everything is better than a lot of nothing. The plan helps me focus and gives me scaffolding on which to balance. It supports me and directs me, and somehow or other, everything always ends up getting done.

I stay calm when faced with too much to do.
I take a few minutes to make a list and a plan.
I do not skip meals or skip sleep. I take a deep breath and begin.

August 31

Love has no other desire but to fulfill itself... To melt and be like a running brook that sings its melody to the night.

—Kahlil Gibran

It's an easy thing for those I love to take advantage of me, and sometimes some of them do, and I let them. And sometimes I set boundaries, and do not let them. But the purest love I know is the one that has the power to take advantage of me, and chooses not to. It is the most surprising thing to be respected and considered, to be protected from the "taking" principle entirely and be given to instead— and not by the induction of guilt or payback, but just because.

What a gift and a blessing! I am startled by it every time.

Just for today, let's all give to others and not worry about what we get or don't get. Let's give without attachment or an agenda. Let's give because it feels good and because we can. Let's leave our egos at home as we go out into the world, and smile broadly from our open hearts.

I am not worried about what I need to get, but concern myself with how I can be most giving. It feels good, and is its own reward.

September 1

The only difference between a good day and a bad day is your attitude.
—DENNIS BROWN

Attitude really is everything. If I have a pleasant, receptive attitude, I can enjoy my entire day. I can travel through it and let it unfold. If I don't burden myself with hostile, dark thoughts and a sense of being "done to" by life, it all goes smoothly. If I trust whatever is happening, if I accept myself and however I am feeling and the circumstances that surround me, then I can have a great day, every day! I can make my whole life an adventure instead of a chore, an opportunity instead of a sentence, a curiosity instead of a judgment, and a blessing instead of a curse.

It's possible. It's available, and there's only one requirement. I have to get out of the driver's seat. I have to let go of my grasping desire for the way I think things *should* go, stop trying to force everything and everybody in my chosen direction, and just let it all be as it is.

I welcome the day!

September 2

The wheel of change moves on.
—Jawaharlal Nehru

Change is unsettling. There is a desire to backpaddle to what we knew and where we have just come from. Even if we didn't like it, it was familiar. Something about the unfamiliar feels dangerous, as if it has the power to topple us entirely, to disintegrate all that we have spent so long getting in order in our lives and in our minds, like a house made of cards. Yet much as we might want to retreat and go back, we cannot. There is nothing to do but to plunge onward, to fumble, and to accept that we are likely to feel uncomfortable for a while.

Change requires great patience and lots of letting go. We have to live through hours of blind discomfort, not understanding, wanting to fix how we feel and knowing there is no fix, only the process, the process … the process of letting go of the familiar and grieving it, and welcoming the new as it unfolds.

I am unsure going forward, but there is no other way to go.

September 3

There is no surprise more magical than the surprise of being loved.
—CHARLES MORGAN

Our wedding was beautiful in all of the ways I didn't expect. The air was thick and unmoving. In Nick's toast, he told a story of Gruff, his new stepfather, transporting a too-big tractor around curvy West Virginia roads in a rainstorm and how he felt afraid and thought it might be best to stop and get off the road. It was scary and dark and the trailer was lurching from side to side. Gruff turned to him and said, "Don't worry, Nick. We'll get through it." And they did. And we will, too, all of us, get through the storms and heat and whatever comes.

Our wedding was the fulfillment of a hope and the promise of a journey to come. It was tearful and joyful. It was too short and just the right amount of time. It was for us and for everyone who came. It was birth and restoration both. It was the middle and the beginning all at once. It was raw and honest and straight from the heart.

I commit to the ongoing journey of authentic love.

September 4

Don't cry because it's over. Smile because it happened.
—THEODOR SEUSS GEISEL

Every ending is a beginning, and every beginning is also an ending. The two are inextricably linked. Life is full of deaths and births and evolution. It's never-ending and nonstop. It's steady and trickling and crashing all around. It's all things connected.

Summer ends and fall begins. We welcome cooler weather but remember the heat. It has become a part of us. Each summer of our lives accumulates to make us the bundle of experiences that we are. And we embody all of it, just like the earth. We grow and grow through seasons like the trees.

I express my gratitude for the summer that has passed,
and I welcome the coming fall.

September 5

I'd rather have roses on my table than diamonds on my neck.
—EMMA GOLDMAN

One of my favorite things to do is to collect growing things that catch my eye while I'm out on a walk. Grasses, wildflowers, weeds, berries...the selection changes with the seasons. I arrange the day's collection in small vases and place them around the house. And these vases restore my soul every time I look at them. The colors and textures inspire me. They remind me that there's more to life than petty frustrations.

And much the same way that I collect these small branches and flowers, perhaps we all choose what we gather and bring home from our wanderings in the world. Let's bring awareness to the things we pick up and the things we carry into our homes when we return from work or from other adventures. Let's choose wisely. Let's be sure to gather and carry those things that inspire feelings of restoration and joy.

I collect things that restore my spirit and fill me with joy,
and the rest I pass by.

September 6

*There are so many people who can figure costs,
and so few who can measure values.*
—AUTHOR UNKNOWN

I live with a certain amount of financial fear, and it weighs me down. The subject of money makes me tense. Every time I get ahead, some unanticipated expense comes along and washes me back. I give money tremendous power in my life. I allow my financial state to affect my mood and my ability to enjoy the day. And yet, I have lived long enough to know that I can survive economically no matter what, with a certain amount of creativity and hard work. It's not a fancy life, necessarily, but it can still be solid and satisfying.

I want to let money be money and keep my perspective. From privilege to bankruptcy, I have always had a roof over my head and food to eat. There is enough. There is always enough. And I can be happy with more ... or with less.

**My happiness is not determined by my bank account.
I enjoy the real riches of my life.**

September 7

Without enough sleep, we all become tall two-year-olds.
—JoJo Jensen

We need our sleep. It restores us and keeps us fresh. But we sacrifice it recklessly. We stay up too late. We indulge our busy minds and lie awake thinking and thinking and thinking. We do not express our emotions in the daytime, and then we clench our teeth at night. We eat poorly, fail to exercise, and deprive ourselves of fresh air. We discount our needs and then wonder why we suffer.

Let's not. Let's take good care of ourselves, as we would a child. We know how children get when they are tired, or hungry, or need to go outside and play. We attend to them so they can feel as comfortable as possible. Don't we deserve the same?

I stop shortchanging myself and honor my needs.

September 8

Our peace shall stand as firm as rocky mountains.
—WILLIAM SHAKESPEARE

I love the mountains. They are rolling and sensuous and nurture those who live in their view. They change color with the light and raise the morning sun. They curve and bend. They are solid and fluid, stalwart, supple, and ever-earthed.

Let's be like the mountains. Let's rise above things, and overlook them, and be beautiful. Let's change fluidly with the light. Let's be inspiring. Let's be sensuous. Let's be grounded and always maintain our magnificent view.

I am beautiful like the mountains, ever-changing, ever the same.

September 9

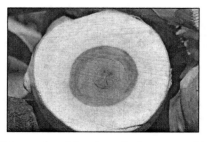

The world is round and the place which may seem like the end may also be only the beginning.
—Ivy Baker Priest

Life is a journey from one thing to the next. The challenge of finding a house to buy becomes getting approved for the mortgage becomes fixing it up, then moving, then adjusting, then the car breaking down, the new job, parental issues, test results, the weather, the children. It never stops. There is always something to test us. We survive one thing and here comes the next. I have wasted so much time wanting to be on the other side of difficulty.

Let's stop projecting beyond the challenge we are facing and find a way to be okay now, no matter what. Let's surrender to the moment and the small joys in front of us, to the unknown, the unseen, and the unexpected. Instead of feeling exasperated and overwhelmed with "Now what?," let's be okay with whatever. Let's say "Why not?" instead of "Why me?" Let's welcome what comes and be willing to experience it … even if we don't understand.

I stop waiting for hardship to end
and accept it as a part of daily living.

September 10

Get mad, then get over it.
—COLIN POWELL

A tremendous amount of anger lurks in the world. I don't like to be angry, and I don't like to be at the receiving end of anger. I don't like raised voices, silent brooding, or violence of any kind. And yet, I have anger within me. I feel it sometimes, lurking, just the way I feel it out in the world.

Anger is a cover story for fear, I think. When I feel afraid, it's because I have no power and no control over something, and I am short on trust. I rage at whatever it is. It's my way of trying to gain control. But instead of getting angry, I can ask myself honestly, "What am I afraid of?" And if I can answer the question, maybe the anger will dissipate; maybe it will shift to tears as it dissolves, or pure exhaustion, or a great big laugh.

I do not contribute to the anger of the world.
I let go of my fear and have compassion for those
who are blindly raging against their own.

September 11

What you need to know about the past is that no matter what
has happened, it has all worked together to bring you to this very moment.
And this is the moment you can choose to make everything new.
—Author unknown

Who we are has more to do with our character than with the
things we have survived. If we throw our traumas before us when
we meet people, we may miss an opportunity to be helpful down
the line. If we introduce ourselves with our names only, and allow
our energy to speak for itself, then we allow others the opportunity
to get to know us as we are, free from our scars. And then over
time, as our relationship evolves, we can slowly share a bit of our
past. We are all survivors of something. It seems like an indication
of great strength to me when I learn that someone I like and respect has been through something horrific and does not lead with
it, does not let it define them. We are alive, first and foremost, in
this day. We have a fresh start. We are not a victim or a survivor
today. We are simply here. We needn't weigh the day down with
long-gone hurts.

Every day I am swept clean.
I can live free from the trauma of my past.

September 12

A book reads the better which is our own, and has been so long known
to us, that we know the topography of its blots, and dog's ears, and can
trace the dirt in it to having read it at tea with buttered muffins.
—CHARLES LAMB

I have made plans to visit a bookstore only to arrive and find the store empty, closed, and utterly abandoned. Gone are the cozy aisles of books, the chairs planted around the floor, the coffee shop and tables, and mostly, the *feeling* ... the feeling of being surrounded by the written word. I drive away disappointed and a bit lost. Are real books doomed like telephone booths? I hope not. For my part, I will seek them out. Slick computer screens and power buttons and rechargeable batteries can bring us only so much satisfaction. They bring us speed, and convenience, and access to everything we could find at any bookstore, but without the character, and without the cozy feeling of sitting in a chair turning real paper pages, and without being surrounded on all sides by aisles and aisles and aisles of books.

I appreciate things in life that have nothing to do with technology.

September 13

Success isn't a result of spontaneous combustion.
You must set yourself on fire.
—ARNOLD H. GLASOW

It's easy to blow off dreams. They seem so impossible, such a stretch … they are *dreams*, after all, even if they call to us. It feels foolish and indulgent somehow to even try for them. It's so much easier to shrug and doubt and be full of sour grapes. It will never work anyway, we tell ourselves, as the years tick away and we have yet to begin. We are kidding ourselves to think we can do whatever it is.

But how can we ever know for sure unless we give it a real shot? And how can we do that if we won't even give it a few hours in our week? It's too easy to make excuses, and they are readily available. But excuses don't make dreams come true. Focus does that, and hard work, and dedication, and a bit of God's grace. Our dreams are worth our effort. Let's give them a chance.

> *If there is something I want to achieve,*
> *I am willing to make time for it.*

September 14

Rejoice in the things that are present.
—MICHEL DE MONTAIGNE

We don't have to project into the future or dwell on the past. If we keep our minds focused on the moment and the day we're in, we can live free from worry. We can live free from fear and grasping. We can be content with and open to whatever the day presents. We don't have to manipulate it and manage it. We can allow ourselves to be surprised by the way it unfolds. We can say please and thank you. We can be grateful just to be alive and to be able to experience it at all. Sun-up to sundown is a rich and simple way to live. It's stress-free and sustainable—good for the spirit, good for the body, and good for the heart.

I live in the day. I am free from worry. I am awake and aware.

September 15

The good life is a process.
—CARL ROGERS

We get through things in life. We are faced with difficult situations. We are faced with extreme and sudden accidents, tragic deaths, debilitating diseases, seemingly insurmountable obstacles, baffling mysteries, and incidents of all kinds. And somehow, against all odds, we make it through them. We make it through our sadness and our rebellion and our fears. We summon up the courage to face what we do not want to face.

We take a step forward, and then another. Our path is revealed to us piecemeal. That's how we get through everything: never more than we can handle, and one little bit at a time. We can try to take it all at once, hoping to get through it more quickly that way, but if we want peace, we will not insist upon seeing or understanding more than life reveals at any one time.

I do not take on more than the day and the moment require.
I am equal to the situation I am in. I don't have to take
the next step until I have to take it.

September 16

God has entrusted me with myself.
—EPICTETUS

Sometimes we have to stop everything and retreat. Sometimes we need to lick our wounds. It's the right thing to do. We are quick to discount our suffering and brush off injury of all kinds. We are willing to ache and be martyrs, or to be tough beyond necessity. We push beyond reason, live on caffeine and not enough sleep, eat poorly, repress our feelings, stay in abusive relationships, speak unkindly to ourselves, and even go so far as to hate ourselves, our lives, and our circumstances. So when, on occasion, we are forced into self-care and self-attendance—after surgery, after an accident, after a breakdown—I believe these times serve as a reminder. We are our own caretakers. How are we doing at that job?

I treat myself tenderly today. I am gentle and loving
and I attend to my needs with care.

September 17

Strangers are just friends waiting to happen.
—ROD MCKUEN

It's easy to hold our feelings and our fears inside of us. We can be mysterious and unreadable. We can be stoic. But if we do not share ourselves with others, we separate ourselves from the very thing that brings us our greatest comfort, and we end up isolated and feeling all alone. We suffer needlessly.

If we open up, if we have the courage to speak about our challenges, others will come forth who have been there before us and made it to the other side. Their stories are our hope. We realize that we are not alone, and that we don't have to go through anything alone, whether it be joyful or scary, or both. And shared experiences are what this journey is all about—getting through things together, getting through whatever comes … and whatever goes. It's a lonely road if we don't open up. Even happiness is diminished if there is no one to reflect it back to us.

I speak up and let others know what's going on with me.

Exaggeration misleads the credulous and offends the perceptive.
—ELIZA COOK

It's important and useful to say, "I'm sorry." If we own our mistakes and acknowledge when we have hurt other people's feelings, whether intentionally or by accident, it allows the energy of forgiveness to permeate our lives, which is healthy and freeing. We can more easily forgive others their wrongs if we are honest about our own. Making a certain allowance for all of us being human and doing the best we can leads to flexible living and generous loving in all of our relationships.

But we can take it too far, and many of us do. Some of us apologize for anything and everything in an effort to keep the peace, and we are accommodating and people-pleasing to a fault. Over-apologizing is seriously problematic and detrimental to our self-esteem. It is falsely humble and makes us unnecessarily pathetic. We hope for appreciation but invite anger and abuse instead, much like a cowering dog.

I stop spilling empty apologies all over the earth.

September 19

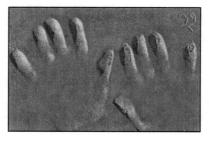

I think everybody should get rich and famous and do everything
they ever dreamed of so they can see that it's not the answer.
—JIM CARREY

Fame is fleeting and relative. An individual can be famous in a town, a school, a country, a family, in certain circles, for a generation, etc. But even those who are famous around the world and across centuries are not known to all. The bottom line is that whether we are known in big circles or small circles, we touch the lives of those whom we are meant to touch, and we are touched *by* others in the same way. We do not need to be famous to be heroic.

Whether we are meant to share our experience with large crowds or a few individuals, we will feel the pull in the right direction. If we are led to fame, so be it. And if we are led to have quiet, private lives and share intimately with only a few, then so be that. There's a plan for all of us, and if we get quiet enough to listen, we will be able to follow the call.

I do not seek fame. I listen for the call of my spirit to action
and pay attention to my inner guidance so that I can
clearly identify where I am supposed to go from here.

Oh, lead me to the beyond within.
—Macrina Wiederkehr

Every so often it's useful to pause and consider the condition of our lives. We get so caught up surviving day to day and handling all that's in front of us that we sometimes lose track of the bigger picture. It's useful to take stock, and look where we are, and appreciate where we've come from. It's useful to ask ourselves some tough questions and be willing to answer them honestly. What needs to change in my life? What am I giving too much of my time to and where am I not giving enough? What can I do without? What can I not do without? How would I live differently if I thought I could get away with it and still pay my bills? Am I happy? Am I healthy? Do I have bad habits? How am I behaving? What am I putting off? What am I doing right? What brings me joy? Do I have a purpose? Am I creatively fulfilled?

Such questions remind us that we have choices and that we are not stuck, even if we feel stuck. Endless possibilities for change abound.

I do not ramble unconsciously through life.
I stop occasionally and take note of where I am.

September 21

Movement is medicine.
—CAROL WELCH

Movement cures many ills. Stiff muscles, distracted minds, pain, fear, and anxiety are all eased by the motion of our limbs. As the blood increases its circulation and we feel the rising warmth of energy within us, the rigid edge of us softens and our tightness releases. Movement helps us discharge worry and stress, uncertainties and frustrations.

But we forget that. We sit and clench and gnaw at our problems and become increasingly annoyed. We have a cocktail and watch television and wonder why we don't feel any better. Our bodies long to move. A quick stretch, a brisk walk—these can alter the entire day's attitude. It doesn't have to be a huge time commitment. Let's just stand up and raise our arms and bend to the side. Let's wiggle a little, and shake, and be playful for just a moment. Let's take the time to move our bodies and relieve our minds.

If I find myself filling with tension,
I take a break from whatever I'm doing and move.

September 22

No road is long with good company.
—Turkish proverb

There is no substitute for spending time with our best friend. Comfort food cannot do it, and neither can movies, naps, walks, massages, or even reading a good book. To exchange knowingness with another occupies its own unique place of delight in life: to share a sense of humor and the light and expression of our eyes; to hug, to tell stories, to be quiet and just occupy space and time together, to prepare a meal, to watch the sunset, the moonrise, to sit on the porch …

My gratitude is for my best friend today, and for all of my friends. They are a blessing in my life, and they enrich my days and my weeks and my whole life experience. How empty life would be without others to share it with!

I am blessed to have friends, and super-blessed
to have a best friend. I show my gratitude with generosity
and compassion and all of my love.

September 23

A light supper, a good night's sleep, and a fine morning have often made a hero of the same man who by indigestion, a restless night, and a rainy morning, would have proved a coward.
—EARL OF CHESTERFIELD

Little creeping irritations can infect a day like termites. They eat at the support beams of good humor. Lack of good sleep, or over-indulgence in food or drink the day before, can contribute to our sensitivity and our sense of angst. Full of sighs and "poor me" thoughts, we are bloated with dissatisfaction and annoyed at all kinds of minor things that ordinarily wouldn't bother us.

If we find ourselves tending in this direction, it's a ringing alarm to wake up and snap back to honesty. Somewhere we have gotten sloppy. We have pushed too far. We have drifted back into thinking we can get by on less self-care than we know we need. We have skimped, or sloughed off, or discounted ourselves somewhere, and there's nothing to do but to acknowledge that we are paying a price for our own poor choices and get back on track.

I choose well so that I can feel well.

September 24

Attitude is a little thing that makes a big difference.
—WINSTON CHURCHILL

What I experience in my day is whatever energy and perceptions are inside of me. If I am dark and brooding, the world appears dark and brooding to me. And if I look out with a loving heart, I see beauty everywhere. A rainy day can be depressing or cozy, depending on my outlook.

If I observe myself being impatient and critical with myself or others, if I feel bitter and resentful, or angry, or jealous, that's a pretty good indication of my level of internal restlessness, and it's a safe bet that I am in need of some attention and self-directed love and care. It's been my experience that in such a situation, there is usually one thing that has triggered the avalanche of darkness, and I am blocked from seeing it or understanding it until I pause long enough to look. But once I have taken the time to see clearly, and once I have touched the primary issue, all of my defenses collapse and it's possible to be relieved and happy once again.

The world does not have to be a certain way for me to be happy.
The quality of my experience is up to me.

The real voyage of discovery consists not in seeking new landscapes,
but in having new eyes.
—MARCEL PROUST

It seems to me that a peaceful and satisfying life requires regular self-reflection to identify whatever issues are blocking us from the light. And then we must be willing to address the issues and change our behavior in relation to them, or our attitude, or both. Quiet and peaceful living is possible and desirable. It does not come from money, or the perfect job, or the perfect relationship, or anything external. It seems to me that it comes from the willingness to make frequent internal adjustments to clear our spirits of the emotional gunk that accumulates, to recognize congestion in the works and strip it clean whenever we need to, and to start fresh, as many times as we need to; to open to the glory of good living, and simple pleasures, and love full up in our hearts.

> ***I'm willing to keep from lugging around***
> ***old and damaging emotional junk.***

September 26

If you surrender to the wind, you can ride it.
—Toni Morrison

When we are young, we are taught the value of effort, the ethic of hard work, and how to set and accomplish goals. But we are less frequently instructed on the disadvantageous results of trying *too* hard. It's a challenge to understand the concept of work without strain. Instead of muscling our way through things and toward our dreams, we can open to the flow of life and let the energy move *through* us instead of pushing our way *against* it.

We must surrender daily on so many levels if we want to experience ease and pleasure. If we are constantly pushing and pushing, we will suffer. We would do best to allow and observe first, and then contribute appropriately as currents permit. Instead of being our own kind of force field, we can learn to recognize our part in the nature of things, and identify what might be dangerous and what might be successful. With practice, we can see and feel the direction in which positive energy seems to be moving, and then make a decision to go with the flow.

I stop trying to force my agenda. I relax and go with the flow.

September 27

The vow that binds too strictly snaps itself.
—ALFRED, LORD TENNYSON

We see a thing partially and believe we are seeing it whole and absolute. We make decisions based on our limited vision and feel good about them, and wise. But when the truth reveals itself to us, when elements of the situation that we have not seen *become* seen, there is no way to go back. What seemed like a solution is suddenly a problem. Our wishful thinking has blinded us to reality.

But once we see clearly, it's important to be honest. It's okay to admit that we've made a mistake and to turn in a fresh direction. We are human. We are supposed to make mistakes. We spend an inordinate amount of time suffering when we refuse to admit our errors, and stubbornly insist that even if something isn't exactly what we hoped it would be, we can still live with it. We convince ourselves that we can make it work … even if it's fairly obvious that we cannot.

It's okay that I make mistakes.
That's what I am supposed to do. That's how I learn.

Falling leaves hide the path so quietly.
—JOHN BAILEY

I love everything about the fall. I love the way the colors start so slowly and then spread and spread and spread until the world is awash with luminosity and fire. I love the fresh mornings and chilly evenings, the first sweaters, the warm covers, the clear air. I love the smell of wood smoke and wet leaves … and dry leaves … and decomposing leaves. I love the sounds of the rustling autumn wind and the Canada geese flying south. I love the way sidewalks and lawns and the edges of streets are lined with red and gold and bright orange.

I love the way fall makes me feel vibrantly alive! It's cozy and fresh at the same time—invigorating and comforting. Old growth is released to the breeze with grace and beauty.

Perhaps, if I bring awareness to my journey, the changes I make in my life and my behavior might be as luminous and spectacular as the trees in fall.

I notice all the sensations the fall season awakens in me
and feel gratitude and joy for the colors and sounds and smells.
I celebrate the wonder of leaves.

Begin at the beginning and go on till you come to the end: then stop.
—LEWIS CARROLL

We get our brains so involved in the situations at hand. We expend time and effort and struggle trying to understand all of the possible implications of a thing, and the future, and the meaning, and on and on. We overthink ourselves into stalemate and anxiety. Let's relax, and trust, and quiet our minds. Let's open to intuition and faith and be willing in every aspect of our lives to wait and see.

I don't overthink my life. I relax, take a deep breath, and live it.

September 30

Truth is tough. It will not break, like a bubble, at a touch; nay, you may kick it about all day like a football, and it will be round and full at evening.
—OLIVER WENDELL HOLMES

I have an avoidance tactic with situations that I don't want to think about or look at. I put on metaphysical blinders. If I don't see something, then surely it cannot be real. With my blinders on, I can be selective about the things I have to face—only those things that I choose to acknowledge. If I don't acknowledge something, then it doesn't exist. The catch and the rub, though, is that it does! It nags and nettles until I *have* to look.

But maybe the ways in which I am potentially vulnerable actually make me beautiful in a way, even as they expose my insecurities. In the final analysis, perfection is boring. It's the imperfect that elicits empathy and compassion and understanding and love. So I'm going to admit my imperfections and face what's true. I'm going to live an honest life, admit my limitations, and not pretend I'm somehow better or healthier or tougher than I am.

I give myself permission to be exactly who I am.

October 1

Sunshine is delicious.
—JOHN RUSKIN

I believe in the healing properties of the sun. I believe we can bathe ourselves in its heat and brightness in moderation to experience maximum health. It soothes my spirit to sit in a ray of sunlight, especially coming through a window on a winter morning or a crisp fall afternoon. It's relaxing and transformative, and to me, it feels endlessly healing. With the warmth on my eyelids, I am carried to other planes of thought and experience. The sun's energy feeds me no less than it feeds the flowers. It penetrates my skin and reaches deep. In a momentary sunbath, I am restored to my purest spiritual state.

***I appreciate the sun today. I take a moment
to express my thanks for its brightness and warmth.***

October 2

Courtesy is a small act but it packs a mighty wallop.
—LEWIS CARROLL

In some ways we are all grabby and insecure. We are too busy, too stressed, too overwhelmed, and too preoccupied to take an extra moment to be polite and genteel with the variety of people we encounter throughout the day.

We surround ourselves with a fortress of technology and can't be bothered with civility. We miss human connections in our lives that could lift our spirits and lighten our loads because we have cellular business to conduct and texts to return. We have to update our status online.

Let's be kind. Let's be considerate. Let's open doors and take note of the people we pass. Let's use our manners and open our hearts. Let's be ladies and gentlemen, starting right now and going forth into the future. Let's restore courtesy to our lives and experience the joys of living with grace.

> *I take the time to be courteous*
> *and slow down enough to be truly considerate.*

October 3

I exist as I am—that is enough.
—WALT WHITMAN

Some people are grouchy by habit. Even when they feel good or happen to be enjoying themselves, they won't admit it because it would blow their whole grouch facade. And perhaps, if we're honest, we are all a little bit that way. We never want anyone to know that we're having too much fun or feeling too good.

Surely it's okay to express our joy and happiness without guilt, and if others don't like it or can't handle it, then that's on them. We don't have to pretend that life is all burden and drudgery and try to somehow prove that we are working harder and struggling more than anyone else. We have value because we are alive, not because of how much we produce or how hard we work. Our life can be an expression of the joy of our existence. It need not be some test of endurance where the one who suffers the most wins.

> *I need not prove my right to happiness.*
> *It is the direct result of my having been born.*

October 4

You are as young as your faith, as old as your doubt;
as young as your self-confidence, as old as your fear;
as young as your hope, as old as your despair.
—General Douglas MacArthur quoting Samuel Ullman

I am convinced that we don't *have* to become old in our thinking or our spirits, or even in our bodies. I believe that in some ways we can be more vital and strong and bright-eyed at eighty-five than we could ever be at thirty.

Most of us seem to arrive on earth wound super-tight, and it takes years and years for us to unwind. But once we do, there is unlimited potential to enjoy our lives. Aging is a journey of fine-tuning, it seems to me. We can *always* be in better shape some-how—physically, mentally, emotionally, spiritually. If we are honest with ourselves about what could use improvement, we can regularly make small changes and alterations that improve the quality of our days.

I believe in the possibility
of ever-increasing vitality and good health.

October 5

A man cannot be comfortable without his own approval.
—MARK TWAIN

There are few things more uncomfortable or stressful than knowing that something in our life isn't working and needs to be
changed, but not being willing to make a change ... yet. We are
successful at convincing ourselves for a time that all is well, but
there comes a point where we can no longer justify the situation,
no matter what spin we put on it. Living in this state of discomfort, knowing that change is called for but resisting it with all that
we have, is excruciating, and we function on a short fuse. We are
irritable and self-pitying. We want to be free of our pain and our
angst, but we don't want to have to *do* anything.

And yet, for all our battle and struggle, the moment we stop
kidding ourselves and agree to do whatever it is that we need to
do, our relief is extraordinary. We are relieved of the burden of
dishonesty and resistance, and the path before us suddenly shines
clear.

> *I'm honest about what's not working in my life,*
> *and I'm willing to change.*

October 6

We don't see things as they are, we see them as we are.
—ANAÏS NIN

Our moods and faces change from the morning to the afternoon, and we are never exactly the same from one day, from one moment, to the next. Our weight fluctuates. Our skin loosens. Our eyes are clear or murky. Our wrinkles evolve. And as we shift our perspective on things, we can be clouded and dark like the mountains at night, or crisp and linear the way the peaks rise from the horizon at first light.

I think we have an expectation that we can achieve a certain "look" that we are pleased with, and then maintain it exactly that way forever. But our bodies and our faces are constantly evolving. There is a daily view, ever-fresh and dynamic. We are as curious and wonderful to live with as the mountains, never the same and always beautiful and new.

I am fascinated by facial expressions and the way we all change visually from day to day, and morning to afternoon.

October 7

I had rather be on my farm than be emperor of the world.
—GEORGE WASHINGTON

Without safety, it's hard to reach our full potential. If our world is filled with nothing but chaos, then we cannot help but falter emotionally, and in every way. But with a solid base, we can grow steadily and with confidence. We can travel and go on adventures and explore broadly in the world knowing that we have a safe place to come home to, a place where we are protected and supported by love.

> *I am grateful for the solid people and things*
> *in my life that make me feel safe.*

October 8

Eliminate physical clutter. More importantly, eliminate spiritual clutter.
—TERRI GUILLEMETS

If I have a big idea, it's often difficult to explain it to people succinctly, so I find it a useful exercise to put pen to paper and write my thoughts down. They begin by being general and scattered, a little bit of this, a lot of that, some here, more there, a pile in the middle. With effort and attention, I can condense the scatter and narrow it down, and then repeat the process, and repeat it again. After a handful of reductions, my real purpose begins to emerge, and eventually, it gets so that I can state my big idea in one concise sentence.

If I find myself confused and befuddled in my emotions, I can do the same thing. I can reduce and reduce and reduce. I can take the time to get to the root of the root, the seed of truth, and the source of my distraction. In attempting to be clear and to easily understand, as in so many other realms of life, less is inevitably more, and simple is best.

I simplify my thoughts and emotions. I say what I mean.

October 9

The only exercise some people get is jumping to conclusions.
—AUTHOR UNKNOWN

One time I tried on an expensive jacket that was tight across the back and the sleeves were too short when I extended my arms. I was told that it shouldn't matter because I wasn't going to be walking around pushing my arms forward, and I could wear it with a thin shirt.

Don't we all do this? When someone tells us they don't want something with a simple "no thanks," we often think they *should* want it, so we check again, and double-check. "Are you sure?" We try to convince them that maybe they *do* want it after all, or that they feel a certain way that they have already told us they don't actually feel. We're not very good about honoring what people tell us and believing they mean what they say. We are too busy, too frenetic, and not mindful enough to really listen and pay attention. When someone tells us no, let's respect that, and not second-guess it out of habit, thinking that we know better. Let's honor each other, and let everybody speak for themselves.

I don't let others talk me into things when I know better.

286

October 10

You may be deceived if you trust too much,
but you will live in torment unless you trust enough.
—FRANK CRANE

I can be enjoying every aspect of my life, full of gratitude and a wholesome sense that all is well, and with one small alteration to my plan or expectation, my mind flips. I go from believing that everything is great to feeling sure that I won't be able to survive. And I am capable of doing this multiple times in the course of a single day.

I know intellectually that everything always works out. My expectation of disaster and punishment is no more realistic or practical than my expectation of a smooth ride with no problems. What happens is not up to me, even if I think it is. There are other factors involved that I cannot foresee or understand. So I can let go of what I can't hold on to anyway, and continue to remind myself as many times as it takes that I can trust the process. It has never let me down yet.

There's always more to it than just me.
I can relax and enjoy the ride.

October 11

Acceptance is the answer.
—BILL WILSON

If it were raining and the rain didn't suit my mood or coordinate with my plan for the day, I could step outside and try to straighten things out. I could say, "Please stop, rain. You are coming down too hard and you are ruining my day." And then, when the rain continued on, I could up the ante. I could say, "That's it! I tried being nice. Now I'm angry and you need to stop. Listen to me or else!" And then I could stomp my feet. I could scream and throw things at the sky, or burst into tears and plead pitifully.

This example may seem silly, but isn't that what we do all the time with people and things in our lives that we want to change? We are sure that if we ask in just the right way, if we master the correct approach, then we can get what we want. But we have no more control over most things than we do over the rain. If we want peace of mind, we have to adjust ourselves to what is, instead of insisting fruitlessly that everything out there has to adjust itself to suit us.

> *I stop battling what is beyond my control*
> *and work on adjusting my attitude.*

October 12

The obstacle is the path.
—ZEN PROVERB

The first time I heard about "enlightenment," it was something I wanted. As a result, my life as a young adult became a quest for spiritual knowledge. I learned how to work with the subtle energies of the body, and I tried meditation on cushions and experimented with all kinds of esoteric practices. Anything and everything has been a part of my path.

And then, one afternoon a few years ago, I was sitting at a traffic light having just left a group meditation session, and a profound thought occurred to me: What if enlightenment wasn't something to "seek" out there in the future after all, some crowning glory of a life well lived, but was something possible and available to me every minute of every day? What if it was a way of seeing and a way of being, and it was as simple as that? I apply my intellect and judgment and logic and good sense. And so often, the very answer I seek, the thing I most long for, is right in front of me, and too obvious for me to believe.

What simple truth am I not seeing?

October 13

A good man is hard to find.
—FLANNERY O'CONNOR

I am married to a good man, and today is his birthday. He is an example of what we could all hope to be. He does not push his will. He refuses to suffocate others, or manipulate them, or overpower them. He is kind and giving and has a sense of humor. He does not take himself too seriously, but is ever-ready to protect what needs protecting. His spirit is gentle but powerful. He is intuitive, allowing, visionary. He is gifted artistically. He can fix anything, create anything, understand anything. He is interested in solving problems. He is low drama and non-combative. He is an excellent communicator. He knows how to calmly share what's going on inside of him and listen to what's going on inside of me. He knows who he is. He is strong and fiercely loving. He lets me be who I am and does not try to change me.

I am blessed to know what it's like to love and be loved.

October 14

Dignity consists not in possessing honors,
but in the consciousness that we deserve them.
—ARISTOTLE

It's not possible to get ahead in life by taking advantage of others, not ultimately. In the short run, advancement and success can result from squashing people, and discrediting them, and bullying them. But sooner or later, the negative action circles back. Call it karma or the law of attraction or justice. Whatever we call it, it never fails to play out ... somehow.

Let's prosper by spreading prosperity. Let's lift others with us as we climb to the top. Let's win by winning, and succeed by having integrity, and rise by doing what's right.

I live by honor and grace.

October 15

Many things grow in the garden that were never sown there.
—Thomas Fuller

Most of us are blocked to love—some of us more so, and some of us less. We are like a garden, and easily overtaken with weeds and vines and out-of-control growth. With attention and time, and the desire to clean things up, we can be clear, but it takes regular maintenance and all the honesty we can muster. We have to be willing to look, and to see, and to cut things away. We have to pare back and uproot what we don't want, and fortify what we want to grow stronger.

Let's be honest about what energy we are expressing. Are we loving? Or are we blocked to love? And if we are blocked, what can we clear away to open ourselves to the light once again?

> *I tend to my inner garden, and I am willing*
> *to do some weeding to neaten things up.*

October 16

As we express our gratitude, we must never forget that the highest appreciation is not to utter words, but to live by them.
—JOHN F. KENNEDY

Gratitude is never bored. Gratitude sees beauty and possibility in everything. It is expansive and all-embracing. It is satisfied and content. Gratitude has compassion for complacency, and understands it as an unhappy internal position, a lingering view of deprivation. Gratitude focuses on abundance instead. It is big-hearted and forgiving.

Let's walk the path of gratitude starting now and going forth. Let's want what we have and appreciate whatever comes. Let's be bigger than complacency, bigger than entitlement, and bigger than boredom. Let's celebrate the bountiful harvest of our everyday life experience.

I wake up every morning with fresh eyes and an open heart.
I am full of wonder and gratitude for my life.

October 17

Chase down your passion like it's the last bus of the night.
—TERRI GUILLEMETS

We can do without coordination, artistic gifts, social graces, money, approval, and even intimacy, but life is a flat experience without heart. We need it. For a life worth living, we need the spirit within us that gets excited over possibilities and is tireless and scrappy and doesn't give up. It's heart that inspires us and heart that keeps us going when the chips are down. It's The Little Engine That Could and Secretariat: the underdogs of the world that come from out of nowhere and blow our minds with their spirit and dedication and ability to do what they should not reasonably be able to do.

But it doesn't have to be as grand and explosive as all of that. It can be as simple as living with enthusiasm. The only thing that limits us is our imagination and age-old fears. Let's feel our fears and go forward anyway! Let's do the things that call to us! Let's give them a shot. We have nothing to lose and a world of experience to gain. Let's do it! Let's live with heart.

I allow myself to get excited about all of the possibilities in my life.

October 18

For after all, the best thing one can do
When it is raining, is to let it rain.
—HENRY WADSWORTH LONGFELLOW

Yesterday on my walk, the air was damp, but chilly and fresh. It was lightly misting, and I enjoyed the fog and the wet world smells. And then it began to rain hard, and I had an initial "oh no" response. I had no rain gear with me. There was nothing to do but walk on and get wet. Our dog, Boss, leaped and splashed through every puddle he could find and got himself covered in mud. Part of me wanted to make him stop so I wouldn't have to deal with cleaning him up, but I couldn't bring myself to discipline him for having such fun.

We collapsed together on a rug in the laundry room when we got home and toweled off. And when we were warm and dry, I felt good. I was happy to have been out in the weather and that I had gotten wet. Every so often, I think it's healthy to get soaked in the rain.

I experience the outdoors and am not afraid to get dirty or wet.

October 19

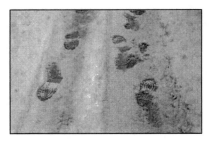

Follow your inner moonlight.
—ALLEN GINSBERG

I believe we are meant to honor the inclinations of our souls. One soul dreams of lounging in a hammock and living life near the sound of waves, and another is driven toward extreme productivity and corporate success. One soul envisions herself dancing in the ballet, and another wants to break the Olympic record for speed skating.

Some dreams are fanciful and do not endure. They "go out" like spring fashions. But others do not go out, and will not leave us, even if we make gallant attempts to ignore them, even if we insist that they go away because they taunt us with their seeming impossibility. These are the longings we must pay attention to. They direct our path and guide the passage of our journey through life. There's something in us that is perfectly fitted to our dreams and visions, and we are meant to acknowledge them, and express ourselves through them, and learn from the places they take us.

I let my dreams guide my steps.

Life is not merely to be alive, but to be well.
—MARCUS VALERIUS MARTIALIS

So much harm occurs under the guise of "fun." We think if we can change the conditions of life with a little chemical help (and I think, if we're honest, we need to put sugar in this category), then all of our worries will be over. But the external "fix" just ends up adding to our mounting list of woes—but not immediately. There is that momentary fulfillment of hope, which is why external pleasure seeking is such dangerous business. It's sneaky, and seductive, and insidious. But in the end, it does nothing but rob us of its spectacular promises.

Real pleasure comes from welcoming life however it comes, and having the faith to trust whatever happens; finding beauty in each day's experience, and recognizing that if we are miserable, we have to make our adjustment on the inside. In the final analysis, there's no such thing as an external fix ... at least, not one that lasts. "On the inside" is where it all happens. "On the inside" is the only place where real happiness lives.

I do not seek my happiness in external things.

October 21

The truth brings with it a great measure of absolution, always.
—R. D. Laing

We've all made bad decisions and mistakes. We've trusted the wrong people and behaved in ways that were reprehensible. We've embarrassed ourselves, spoken when we should have remained quiet, thrown our energy in all the wrong places, been jealous, resentful, and riddled with doubt. Our fallibility surrounds us like ripples on a lake. If we admit to our mistakes, we relate easily to others and others to us. We can laugh at our own ridiculousness. But if we keep our mistakes locked up inside and make the assumption that everyone else is different and somehow better, we isolate ourselves unnecessarily.

Let's be honest about ourselves as whole people and be okay as we are, with all of our past wrongdoings and crazy thoughts. Let's stand square on the earth with our heads up, with no guilt and no shame, free and clear and in the light.

I have the courage to share my whole self with others.
I am not afraid to be imperfect.

*Everyone takes the limits of his own field of vision
for the limits of the world.*
—ARTHUR SCHOPENHAUER

There's more than one way to do anything. We get so caught up thinking our way is the "right way," but it's not necessarily. It may be the right way *for us*. But we have to allow others their creativity and particular way of seeing things, and allow for the very real possibility that they may have a fresh perspective on the situation that could be beneficial all the way around.

It's not infrequently that I find myself shutting down someone else's idea or suggestion before it has even been fully expressed. It's important for me to remember to be open to all possibilities and be willing to be flexible. I wonder why I am always so quick to push and struggle and force things to happen without taking additional options into consideration. I seem so anxious to form my opinion, to get things done, and to shut the door. What's my big rush?

**My way is not the only way,
but it's the only way that I can see.**

October 23

To every thing there is a season,
and a time to every purpose under heaven.
—ECCLESIASTES 3:1

The routine of days carries us onward like leaves floating down a creek. We end up downriver and wonder how we got there so soon. It's a real challenge to learn how to determine what matters most and then to prioritize properly, and to focus on the task at hand without feeling frazzled about the tasks awaiting, and to make time for relaxation and laughter and good eating and exercise and intellectual stimulation and walks in the outdoors.

We must find the proper balance between choosing to do for others and choosing to do for ourselves, and not rush and not worry. There is time for work and time for play; for dreams and achievement and lounging and sleep, for books and movies and conversation and the news, for changing moods and singing for joy, for hugs and travel and tears and faith. We have to remember that there is enough time for everything that matters.

I relax about having enough time.
I enjoy the flow of days and seasons.

October 24

The bamboo that bends is stronger than the oak that resists.
—JAPANESE PROVERB

The world is ever-changing, and so are we, and so are others. But we seem to resist that fact, and insist upon our certainties. We insist upon our beliefs. We make assumptions that the present situation will be the same way that something similar was in the past, and that it will affect us the same way. But it doesn't, even though we might react as if it does. And we assume people will be the same way they were in the past as well, but people can change, too, and soften over time … or harden. Perhaps life cycles around in the way it does in order to show us exactly how *we* have changed, for better or worse, if we are aware enough to even notice. Everything is variable, and relative. So there's no glory or percentage in being stubborn and unbending, hard-headed and close-minded. Strength without flexibility is breakable, and not really worth much in the end.

I make room in my life for changing points of view
and allow for shifts in my belief system from one day to the next.

October 25

You can only come to the morning through the shadows.
—J.R.R. TOLKIEN

Some mornings I pop out of bed full of energy and ready for the adventure of the day. Other mornings come less easily. It is an effort to get up and get moving. I'm like a fire that has gone a bit too far into the ember stage overnight, and requires extra twigs and billowing to reignite. There is a bit of smokiness initially, and a stubborn refusal to burst forth. But eventually, the flame rises and the smoke recedes and I am off and running yet again.

When motivation is lacking, the only approach I know is to keep on moving, to go through the go through, to do the next right thing, and then the next, the best I can, even if my brain is murky, even if my muscles ache. And inevitably, the spirit engages, and energy rises within, and I warm into the day in stages, until I feel fully alive and happy yet again.

If the day comes at me hard, I just go through the motions and trust the momentum of my movement to carry the spirit, until the spirit can take over and carry the day.

October 26

The words you choose are just as important as the decision to speak.
—AUTHOR UNKNOWN

"Yes, but ..." are slippery words. We agree to something with reservations. If there is a "but" clause, perhaps we had just better say no instead. We want to have it both ways by saying yes with conditions, but that's not entirely straight up. If our "yes" or our "no" is actually a "maybe," then we need to say so. The "but" caveat is our allowance to whine and complain, to make sure it's known that we are willing to do something but we are not happy about it. There's a "poor me" echo in "yes, but ..." It's dishonest in a way. It's not a real yes.

The world is confusing because we all are so frequently unclear about our meaning. We tell people what we think they want to hear instead of telling them the truth. Let's bring awareness and care to what we are saying. Let's say yes when we mean yes, and no when we mean no. It sounds simple, but it's not. We confuse the two all the time, and end up bitter and resentful. We feel used and misunderstood, but the error is ours.

I bring awareness to the words I use, and I say what I mean.

October 27

Become conscious of being conscious.
—ECKHART TOLLE

If a stampede is coming across the plains, we might feel an internal thrill as we puff out our chest and resolve to stand tall against it. But it's entirely possible, even though we resolve to stand up against it, that we may not be able to. It *is* a stampede after all. We could get flattened or seriously injured. And what horror, either way, to be among the crush of hooves! But we *could* step out of the way. We could feel the distant vibration in the earth and get ourselves to high ground. And from there, we could watch.

Just so, we have a choice whether to participate in emotional stampedes, and to participate in our own mental stampedes of worry and fear. We can move to high ground. We can watch and wait and be curious. From high ground, we can see when the danger has passed and it's safe again to move around.

I am willing to be an observer of life's drama. I don't always have to be in the middle of it all pushing against the fray.

October 28

This is the day the Lord has made; let us rejoice and be glad in it.
—PSALM 118:24

Whether we admit it or not, we are all alive and living not by our wit, or even by our intuition, but entirely by grace. Our lives are fragile beyond our wildest imagination, and can be taken from us in an instant for no particularly good reason. When our time is up, it's up, and we have no control over when and how.

Life is a gift, and one that we cannot take for granted. It's naive to expect that we have years ahead of us in which to make better choices and pursue our dreams. We can't wait to be kind, to be forgiving, and to show our love. If we want to be loving, we have to be loving *now* ... or fit, or gentle, or well read. This is the time. This is the day.

Let's be grateful for all that we have been given, for all of our blessings and the beating of our hearts. Let's bubble over with thanksgiving for the grace that keeps us going, and make the most of it. Let's wake up and enjoy the day.

I don't know about tomorrow or next week or five years from now. I appreciate this day.

October 29

Silence is a source of great strength.
—LAO TZU

I always have a choice to experience inner quiet, although it doesn't always feel like I do. I am so good at creating little dust storms of flurried activity and mental anguish. I think I have to move faster to make it stop, that getting every single little thing done will make it stop. But the only thing to do is to stop *me*, to sit for five minutes and remember what I'm all about, and what matters. I can pause amid all the activity and take a deep breath. I can make a conscious effort to shift my energy and regroup internally. The external stuff is just stuff. I've given it power and importance that it doesn't actually hold. After pausing, I can move on refreshed and full of better, calmer, more stable energy—energy that is actually far more productive in the end.

I catch myself in an internally frantic mode and stop moving.
I restore balance and regain perspective
before I continue with my day.

October 30

Wisdom consists of the anticipation of consequences.
—Chinese proverb

It's easy to get caught up in the moment and make allowances for things without properly considering the costs of our choices. Against our better judgment, we make a split-second decision to act, figuring that just this one time, surely, it can't hurt. We have a sense of being invincible—that we can lift something ridiculously heavy, or stay up all night, or get soaking wet in freezing weather with no way to dry off, or over-eat desserts.

But the piper comes and he always demands his pay. It may seem that we have gotten away with something, that we have skirted through completely free of negative consequences. We feel smug and righteous. So no one is more surprised than we are when the bill arrives. We wonder how it happened. We feel unhappy and full of regret. Sometimes it's sooner and sometimes later, but the dues for our choices always have to be paid.

I refrain from impulsive action and remember
that for every decision I make, there is a consequence.
Poor decisions exact a high cost.

October 31

At first cock-crow the ghosts must go
Back to their quiet graves below.
—THEODOSIA GARRISON

What haunts us? Which spooks and goblins rattle our nerves? Is it specters from the past or ones from the future that jump out at us from behind dark corners and terrify us when we least expect it? Let's put on our brave masks and heroic costumes and face our ghosts. Let's welcome them and give them treats. Let's admire the way they are dressed up, and recognize that underneath they are probably not so scary after all. Let's honor the things that haunt us and then send them on their way.

I am willing to face the ghosts that haunt me.

November 1

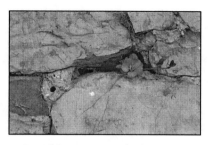

By yielding you may obtain victory.
—Ovid

Horrible happenings in my life have turned out to be great blessings, and the most difficult people have been my best teachers. Knowing this, I have no need to fear whatever I am currently experiencing. I can be full of trusting curiosity. But I'm not, or not always. I seem to revert to an expectation of punishment and disaster.

I want to become ever more grounded and solid in the faith that all is well, and all is always well, and happening on time, and for a reason, and that it's all going to be just what it's supposed to be. If it's tough, if it's dark, if it feels impossible, then what a blessing! I will grow in depth. I want to have gratitude while it's happening instead of only in looking back. I want to have that kind of faith and that kind of trust. I want to know and believe all the way to my core that whatever happens is going to be okay, and is going to be okay with me. I want to trust the process beyond a shadow of a doubt.

I am willing to be okay with things the way they are.

November 2

Man is the only kind of varmint sets his own trap,
baits it, then steps in it.
—John Steinbeck

We judge others pretending we have not done exactly the same thing we are condemning. We trip and stumble, and we pull ourselves up and act as if we have never stumbled at all. We worry over the future as if our worrying will give us control. We do not admit to our crazy thinking or to any darkness within us. We take ourselves seriously and believe our own lies.

Being able to laugh at ourselves and at life may be one of the most important features of a satisfying life experience. It's refreshing to be able to smile at our futile efforts and social posturing, our fragile egos, our false pride, and our false humility. Authentic living has to include a sense of humor. Without one, we are kidding ourselves.

I acknowledge and enjoy my part in the silliness of human drama.

November 3

The female contains all qualities and tempers them,
She is in her place and moves with perfect balance,
She is all things duly veiled.
—WALT WHITMAN

In our fast-paced, achievement-driven culture, I think we regularly undervalue the feminine. We're all about the masculine virtues of action and pride, of pushing and striving and manifesting, for both sexes, and not so much about the gentle and quiet, the soft-spoken and sweet, the compassionate and intuitive. Our devaluation of the feminine is a great loss for us all.

Let's lose our hard edges and allow ourselves to be gentle, with both ourselves and others. Let's be nurturing. Let's wrap ourselves up with love and good mothering and the wisdom of the crone. Let's remember that we are all made of both yin and yang, masculine and feminine. We are not one or the other exclusively. We are the perfect combination and the perfect mix.

I value the quiet and enduring feminine energy in me
and in the world.

November 4

When you are sorrowful look again in your heart, and you shall see
that in truth you are weeping for that which has been your delight.
—KAHLIL GIBRAN

For every experience of gratitude and grace, there is an equal portion of hardship and loss. They exist together like the rises and dips of waves. The deep ache of primal grief consumes us utterly and then recedes like the tide. And joy fills us up so that we feel we will always be full with it, and then it empties. Both of them ebb and flow, and life goes on.

Over time, the rushing surges of grief become more gradual, and we learn to assimilate our losses. But it's important to recognize that we are sad still in subtle ways, and that sadness has a kind of permanent place in us. It cannot be pushed out with forced gaiety or affirmations or cheer. It recedes, and joy floods forth. And today's bursting joy becomes dull and foggy, but the echo of it lives on in us and has *its* place. Both of them come and go, and come and go, and in the experience of one is the shadow of the other. They each have their part in the rhythm of life.

> *I honor the sadness in me as well as the joy.*
> *Together they make me whole.*

November 5

The most I can do for my friend is simply be his friend.
—HENRY DAVID THOREAU

How can we possibly feel happy if someone we love is suffering? It feels like the worst kind of betrayal. We are sure that we, too, must suffer, and we do. But perhaps we do not truly honor them by piggybacking on their hard time. Perhaps the best way to demonstrate our compassion is by remaining steady ourselves, and by continuing to enjoy the pleasures life affords us, and by being present—absolutely and completely present—to listen, or entertain, or just to sit; to not become so flustered and discombobulated ourselves that we cannot be of service.

When people we love have lost their anchor and are bobbing around unsure, the thing they need is not for us to pull up our own anchor and bob about with them in sympathy, but to stay grounded and reach out.

I respond to the suffering of others with earthed energy. I do not react with impulsive fears and frenzies that match their own.

November 6

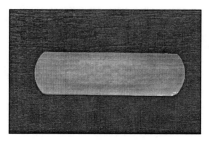

*Our own physical body possesses a wisdom
which we who inhabit the body lack.*
—HENRY MILLER

I can be overly worried about my body sometimes—worried that I might hurt myself or feel pain, or that I am going to get some terrible disease. And yet I have put in the time and effort to build physical strength in myself, and balance, and flexibility, and endurance, and I maintain healthy habits. What else can I do? Like a guy who owns a muscle car and always keeps it in the garage covered with a cloth, I have times when I am afraid to drive. But I need not be. It's my mind stopping me more than my body. I am okay. The thoughts I have about my body can be a powerful ally or my worst enemy. I need to remember that I have a choice.

*I stop talking myself into physical aches and pains
and trust my body to be well.*

November 7

*What lies behind us and what lies before us
are tiny matters compared to what lies within us.*
—RALPH WALDO EMERSON

Subtle but powerful energy runs through us and around us. If we could see it, it might appear like heat waves over a desert highway in the summertime. The energy can be radiant or diminished, clear or cloudy, loving or vengeful, hot or cool. It is constantly shifting. Laughter shifts it, as does anger, exercise, food, conversation, stress, and delight. This energy affects us deeply, every day, in every way, even if we are not necessarily aware of it.

It's an important part of our life journey to bring consciousness to the presence of this energy in ourselves, in others, in nature, and in everything living in the world. There may be nothing more valuable that we could turn our attention to—not finances or clothing or being right. Let's awaken to the experience of the living life force within us!

I pay attention to the shifting energy within me and around me.

November 8

*Martyrdom has always been a proof of the intensity,
never the correctness, of a belief.*
—Arthur Schnitzler

There are things in life that we all have to do in order to be contributing members of society, and of our families, and with our friends, and they are not always easy or fun or what we particularly *feel* like doing. We have duties and responsibilities. But some of the things I feel duty-bound to do are actually rooted in my desire to have control.

I get exasperated thinking that others cannot do for themselves, and that nothing will get done *properly* unless *I* do it. In truth, of course, others are entirely capable of doing for themselves, but I don't let them, because I am too busy getting involved in their stuff with all of my opinions and good ideas and volunteering my time.

I am honest about the fact that sometimes my offering to help is less about helping and more about wanting to take control.

November 9

As we are human, we can't do what we can't do;
as we're neurotic, we can't do what we can.
—MIGNON McLAUGHLIN

We think our way into big deals. We are faced with something straightforward and relatively simple, and because of mental associations, projections, and fearful implications, we overcomplicate it to the point of procrastination and avoidance and sometimes even paralysis. We make it out to be something so much more than it is. We are sure that our world and our future and our happiness are all dependent on this one small task, or big task, or whatever it is. We magnify the meaning, when often there is no meaning at all, only a process, and a next step. It's all happening in the course of life. How often have we put something off only to do it at last and be amazed by the ease of simply *doing* it? The mental angst and strain we put on ourselves and carry with us in the shadow of things undone is ridiculous and unnecessary.

> **My mind can make a big deal out of anything,**
> **even if it's no big deal.**

Perception is a clash of mind and eye, the eye believing what it sees,
the mind seeing what it believes.

—Robert Brault

What is "the truth"? Who has the right to determine it? And is there one absolute truth, or is truth relative and dependent on different points of view? We impose personal meaning onto things that are effectively neutral. Our perception is our personal truth, but we have to allow that the same thing may be perceived very differently by others. And sometimes our truths may be in conflict with each other, and sometimes they may not. The truth is not as simple as it initially appears. Life is mysterious, and there is so much we don't know and can't understand. Maybe that's the only real truth we can hold on to in the end.

I am willing to honor your truth as well as my own
and allow for the possibility that even if we disagree,
we may both somehow be right.

November 11

Beauty is a light in the heart.
—KAHLIL GIBRAN

The positive attention we direct toward others is like sunshine on a cold day. We can warm the chill of someone's experience with a smile or some other kind of small recognition. If we open our eyes and our hearts, we can see the beauty in people. We can see their potential and believe in them even when they don't believe in themselves—maybe especially then. There is incredible power in the words "You can do it!" We can frame things in a positive way. We can point out what's wonderful in others, and the things they do well.

The ripple effect of these small acts of kindness is that *we* end up feeling good. We are warmed by smiles in return. So let's do it. Let's pay attention to people, and love them just because. Why not? We have nothing to lose and everything to gain. Life is short and hard. Let's spread whatever joy we can.

I notice people today and think well of them.
I focus on what's beautiful.

November 12

If you fall in the mud puddle, check your pockets for fish.
—AUTHOR UNKNOWN

It's unrealistic to think I can find a way to always be happy. It's natural that I should shift back and forth from clarity to blindness, from love to fear. And yet I seem unable to take them both in equal stride. I welcome the bright side and resist the dark with all I have. But, if I'm honest, some of my greatest spiritual evolution has come to me by way of the muck and the murk. There is great value in the muddy puddles and swampy bogs of life. I suppose it's unlikely that I could ever actually *embrace* the difficult passages of life, but maybe I can learn to stop fighting them. And instead of being irritated with feeling less than perfect, perhaps I can learn to say, "Ahh, here I am again. I know this place, and know it will pass, and until it does, I will let it be here and trust the lessons that it has to teach me."

I fully enjoy feeling good,
and I'm open to the experience of feeling less than good.

November 13

There is more to life than increasing its speed.
—Mahatma Gandhi

The energy of my life is uncomfortable when I am in a rush. Anyone who is not moving as fast as I am is a source of immediate frustration. I am easily exasperated and tough to please. When I am relaxed, I simply witness whatever is happening around me and feel at ease. I notice other people rushing and commend myself for not being one of them. I enjoy the simple details of the environment.

Rushing doesn't make anything happen any faster except for the depletion of my energy and patience, so there's really nothing intelligent about it, no matter how I look at it. The truth is that I can be efficient and streamlined and steady without *having* to rush. I can slow down. I can relax about things. I can get in the habit of allowing myself extra time, or, if there is no extra, I can savor the time that I have.

Life is too precious to rush through it. I am willing to slow down.

November 14

The most beautiful thing we can experience is the mysterious.
—ALBERT EINSTEIN

There's a difference between contemplation and analysis. Contemplation feels gentler. It wanders and is willing to be unsure. It asks open-ended questions and leaves things up for discussion. Analysis, on the other hand, seeks certainty. It wants to categorize and pigeonhole. It wants to tie things up with a string and put them away: done, solved, next. Its approach is cut-and-dried, hard-edged. It seeks to solve, not to wonder.

I bring both energies to my life, but I prefer the contemplative. I get in trouble when I try too hard to figure things out. I suffer needlessly asking "Why this?" and "Why that?" and needing to understand. Instead I can ask "Why not?" I can think "perhaps" and "let's see" and "What about this over here?" Contemplation allows for all possibilities. I don't have to solve anything or come to any conclusions. I can wander playfully in and around the ramblings of my spirit and my mind.

I honor the living curiosity within me that wants to explore.

November 15

As your faith is strengthened ... things will flow ...
and you will flow with them, to your great delight and benefit.
—Emmanuel Teney

I cannot get what I want in life by grabbing for it. If I try too hard, I block the flow of energy and end up stuck. Everything in life is come and go and the law of attraction. What I send out comes back to me. If I am rigid with the fear of "not getting," then "not getting" is what I manifest. If I am trusting and loving and confident, then that's what shows up in my life. I have to give it away to keep it and let go to be able to hold on. My agenda is not nearly as important as my faith.

I am open to the possibility that I may not get what I think I want,
but I am willing to trust what I get.

November 16

*My cup runneth over. Surely goodness and mercy shall follow me
all the days of my life.*

—PSALM 23

I am grateful for the cozy feeling of thick socks. I am grateful for
walks and the way it feels to stretch. I am grateful for bananas and
eggs and toast and molasses and pancakes. I am grateful for bis-
cuits. I am grateful for fresh mornings and the color of dusk, for
rain and snow and sunshine, for gentle breezes and possibility and
hope. I am grateful for books and wood smoke and candle-light. I
am grateful for sleep, and for waking up.

One thing leads to another. Our gratitude can start anywhere
and grow from there. And as it grows, it fills us with good feelings. So let's take the time. Let's make it a daily practice to celebrate and acknowledge our blessings.

I express my gratitude for the blessings in my life.

Our technology has exceeded our humanity.
—ALBERT EINSTEIN

With our cell phones in hand, we miss out on mysterious adventures and the experience of patiently waiting. We miss out on each other. It makes me sad to see people with a spare moment spending it on texting messages or surfing the web. Maybe we are *too* in touch these days—too closely in touch with each other and with all of our personal projects and activities. It's all so close to us. We can never get away. We have lost the ability to daydream. We rarely sit quietly and look around. We are losing ourselves in cyberspace.

Let's take ourselves back. Let's put down our cell phones and give ourselves a break. Let's spend an hour each day being absolutely free from technology and open to the possibilities of silence and nature and the fresh air. Or we can spend more than an hour, or less, or as much time as we can, so that we don't fill every possible gap with the noise of busyness and end up losing touch with what matters the most.

I leave my cell phone at home and take a walk.

November 18

Oftentimes, when people are miserable,
they will want to make other people miserable, too. But it never helps.
—LEMONY SNICKET

I dislike sarcasm. It cuts and bites and belittles. The original etymology of the word means "to tear flesh," and that's what sarcasm does. It is ripping and shredding guised as good times. My sense is that sarcastic people are angry people. They seem to take a certain pleasure in making others squirm. What is meant to be funny feels more like torture. Humor that comes from an open heart—that pokes fun at itself and others in a gentle and playful way, lovingly, and with kindness—is far more palatable.

Let's bring higher awareness to the way we interact with others, and the bend and curve of our humor. Are we expressing love and appreciation, or judgment? Are we gentle or cruel? Is our laughter full of joy and relaxation, or does it bite? It makes a difference. It makes a difference in the quality of our lives and in the world.

I keep my humor light and gentle.
I avoid teasing, and sarcasm, and laughter that stings.

November 19

What humbugs we are, who pretend to live for Beauty,
and never see the Dawn!
—L. P. SMITH

What is spiritual is actually obvious. It is right before us in the light of day. And somehow we miss it. We look for it everywhere but where it is—in small acts of kindness, and the morning sky, in the tastes and textures of a delicious meal, and the comfort of our beds. Enlightenment is not some kind of "out there" possibility designed only for monks and the seriously meditative. It is available to us all, every minute of every day. It is relaxed awareness and absolute presence. It is free and simple and pure and accessible. It is the joy of being and the realization that we are ever-blessed with a multitude of simple pleasures and surrounded on all sides by extraordinary beauty.

I quiet my mind and appreciate all of the little things in
life ... which are actually the big things, if the truth be told.

November 20

Knowledge will not acquire you; you must acquire it.
—SUDIE BACK

My fears are like certainties until I have spoken with someone who actually has facts and reliable information and experience. But I can never be absolutely sure that the information I receive is free of motivation to steer me one way or the other, so I speak to at least two people who are in the know. And once I've done that, I have a context in which to consider, and I feel less afraid.

We spend so much time in life unsure, speculating on outcomes and projecting disaster. It's unquestionably better all the way around to gather the information we need and then choose the best path we can, and let it play out as it does, rather than driving ourselves crazy with not knowing and second-guessing, and becoming frazzled by the stress of indecision. Reassurance is available to us if only we will seek it out.

> *I ask questions and gather information so that*
> *I can make the best possible choice.*

November 21

I would not waste my life in friction
when it could be turned into momentum
—FRANCES WILLARD

We can't let our aches and pains paralyze us. The answer to almost anything that ails us is movement and action and forward motion. We need mental and physical distraction from our misery and suffering in order to find relief. Nothing exacerbates an unpleasant condition more than focusing on it exclusively. We are less incapacitated by our discomfort than we think.

Let's get up and get out. Let's stretch and walk. Let's dance. This is not a permanent fix by any means, but we can feel better for a little while, and that's worth something. Let's rise above our ailments and move ahead in spite of them. We can take the time we need to be tender and compassionate with all of the ways we hurt, but we cannot wallow in our pain or we will drown. At some point or other, we have to make the decision to pick ourselves up and carry on.

When I am in pain, I take the time I need to rest and heal,
and then I get on with the activity of living my life.

November 22

*People are crying up the rich and variegated plumage of the peacock,
and he is himself blushing at the sight of his ugly feet.*

—SA'DI

Shame is toxic and debilitating and more active in our lives than most of us realize. We do not feel equal to life. We are stumbling and clumsy, embarrassed and awkward. It's sad that any of us should feel shame-bound in the slightest, that we should feel *wrong* in any way for choosing what we have chosen. We are each unique, beautiful, and gifted in our own right.

We all have a role in the distribution of shame as well as the experience of it. Let's watch out for our tendency to judge and fingerpoint. Let's be more inclined to say "Good for you!" than "Why are you doing *that*?" Let's catch shame in the act and send it packing. Let's rejoice in all the different ways we can make our way through life, none of them wrong or better or anything—just choices and experiences and powerful inclinations from the gut.

> *I don't distribute shame or take it in.*
> *I am willing to live life shame-free.*

November 23

Act as if what you do makes a difference. It does.
—WILLIAM JAMES

Many years ago, my sister swallowed three bottles of ibuprofen and chased them with bubble gum–flavored Benadryl. Then she lay down on the floor between her futon and the wall in her apartment in Lander, Wyoming, and slowly died. She left an organ donor card on the kitchen table, but no one found her for three days, and by then, her organs were not salvageable, and neither was she. I'm not sure that she ever understood or appreciated her worth. Maybe things could have gotten better for her, or maybe not. I'll never know.

It's easy to assume that everyone we encounter is doing just fine, especially if we are all wrapped up in our own personal drama. But maybe not. Maybe a smile or a word of encouragement is just the thing someone needs today to change their world and maybe even save their life. We never know how our small acts can affect the quality of someone else's experience.

I don't know how people are hurting.
I spread kindness instead of criticism.

November 24

I heard the teardrop hit my pillow before I even knew I was crying.
—TERRI GUILLEMETS

Let's recognize when something is amiss within us, and then be willing to wait for understanding, which may or may not come quickly. For me, when it does come, it's usually in a kind of conversational purge. I don't want to say something, and then, like a pressure cooker, the pressure builds until I cannot hold it in anymore. I blurt it out, and then another thought follows, and another, sometimes mixed with tears and emotions I didn't even know I had inside of me. And then, I feel better.

I am learning to trust the process of working through things. I have always wanted to handle situations, be past them, get over them, and move on. But the hard emotional stuff inside of me bubbles up in little bits at a time, and has to be processed the same way: slowly, sometimes almost surreptitiously, and steadily ... steadily as it comes up.

I don't blame others for what's going on inside of me. I trust the working-through process and wait for the ability to understand.

November 25

*If the only prayer you said in your whole life was,
"thank you," that would suffice.*
—MEISTER ECKHART

This is the time of year to actively practice gratitude, to acknowledge those things in life for which we are grateful, and to do something to demonstrate our level of appreciation. It is not enough to simply *feel* grateful, although that's a good start. If we appreciate our cars, we can keep them clean and properly maintained. If we appreciate our health, we can take care to eat well and get enough sleep, and to stretch and exercise and not overdo. If we appreciate our spouses, and our children, and our parents, then we can be loving to them, and thoughtful. We can be considerate and extra-kind. The way we behave toward things and people shows our appreciation for them, or our disregard. We are blessed in so many ways. Let's actively demonstrate our thanks.

> *I give thanks for my life's blessings
> and show my appreciation through action.*

November 26

Tomorrow is always fresh.
—L. M. MONTGOMERY

Peering into the unknown future can be unsettling. It's the "unknown" part of it that is disconcerting. We feel sure that if we only knew what was going to happen, then we would feel better. But maybe we wouldn't. I can think of numerous instances where, if I had known what was coming, I might have opted out.

It's important to remember, when wondering what might come, that with the right attitude, any hardship can become an opportunity, and usually does. When faced with seemingly insurmountable situations, we can remain hopeful. We can watch and wait and be amazed as everything works itself out and is restored to balance yet again. We grow in spurts, and then settle in. That's the rhythm and the stretch and the dance of our lives.

> *I am at peace with the unknown.*
> *I welcome the adventure of my future.*

November 27

Joy is not in things; it is in us.
—RICHARD WAGNER

We miss life's essential purpose and pleasures by being too busy. We are too busy in our minds as well as our activities. We work ourselves into a mental and physical frenzy of exhaustion. We think too much, eat too much, work too much, and spend too much. We figure that if a little bit is good, then more must necessarily be better. We strive for more success, more understanding, more perfection, more happiness, and more peace. And in our striving, we completely miss what we already *are* and what we already have, which is more than enough to bring us all the happiness and joy that is possible on earth.

Everything we need, we have within us. We are already perfect. We are whole and complete just the way we are. The purpose of life is to live it, and the reason for being is to be. And if we truly accept that, just as it is, then our satisfaction is so rich and full that it brings tears to our eyes ... and we want for nothing. We are full at last!

I rejoice in the gifts of the moment.

November 28

A good stance and posture reflect a proper state of mind.
—MORIHEI UESHIBA

There are spiritual, mental, emotional, and physical components to good posture. It requires a strong core, self-confidence, a positive outlook, and a right-sized view of our place in the world. We are not meant to crouch and hunch. We are meant to stand upright and be joyful. But as we perceive life happening to us, our shoulders cave in. We become victims of the metaphysical weight of our lives. We curl forward in an effort to protect ourselves, and then we curl forward out of habit. But we needn't. No matter how bowled over by life circumstances we have become, we can learn to straighten up.

Good posture is better for our sense of well-being, better for our bones and muscles, our neck and back, for opportunities in life, and relief from pain. And it's better for aesthetics as well. We look more attractive and younger when we stand up, and we feel that way, too.

It feels good to stand tall, and I'm worth it.

November 29

There is a great fire in our soul ...
and the passers-by see only a wisp of smoke.
—Vincent van Gogh

While brute force is combative and striking, it is limited. It's like a hard slap. It does not have the staying power of our gathered-up inner strength. And yet we spend most of our time using just this force, trying to push at things. We slap at life. We are unsure how to make good use of the unlimited supply of power within us. We "try" weakly at things and fail. We whimper and make excuses. We are full of "I can't" and "It's too hard," but we can, and it isn't!

Let's engage our power when we need it. Let's gather our breath and build it inside of us like fire. It starts low, like a soft and steady drumbeat, and builds, and builds, and builds: louder, stronger, louder, stronger. Let's amp it up and explode it forth! It's possible and it's fun to experience even an inkling of the strength that we store in our depths. This power is available to us always, and is as close as our very breath.

I gather the power available within me
and use it to light up my life.

November 30

Losing weight is not a cure for life.
—Phillip McGraw

Perhaps, as much as anything, our "weight" is the state of our minds. We can feel both full and hungry at the same time. We can be thin and feel fat, or be fat and feel thin. "Light" and "heavy" are fundamentally spiritual concepts, after all, and how we feel, and how we feed ourselves, with either abusive excess or tender loving care, matters in the big picture. Everything is interrelated: our sense of well-being, our level of exhaustion, our food choices, our happiness, our levels of guilt and shame, our triggers, our indulgences, and our misunderstandings. If we want to feel healthy and happy in our bodies and our minds, we must be honest about the motivations that drive us toward better health or away from it. Mastery of diet and body image is not a destination point, it's an ongoing journey of honesty. To live sanely in a world of endless dietary choices, we must learn to honor the emotion-consumption connection.

I'm honest with myself about the reality of what and how I eat.

December 1

Your body is a beautiful manifestation powered by spirit.
—MIKE DOLAN

I have been frustrated with my elbows lately. The protruding bones seem to catch and bump on everything. And yet, they bend and straighten my arms! They allow for hugs and planks and dancing and writing and lifting things. How limited my range of motion and activity would be without them. My elbows are no less than miracles of design and engineering, and my ankles and knees and hips and wrists and fingers are no less: all of my moving parts are no less!

Let's celebrate the wonder of our joints and stop sending them frustrated, negative thoughts. Perhaps they ache a bit … but do they function? Let's find our gratitude. Let's be grateful for our rotators and hinges, for the hardware of our bones, and for our muscles and tendons that move them. We take our bodies for granted. We abuse them with our choices and then gripe when they react. Let's not gripe today. Let's take a moment to appreciate them just the way they are. Our bodies are fantastic and miraculous in every way!

I am grateful for all of my moving parts.

December 2

Don't look for your dreams to come true;
look to become true to your dreams.
—Michael Beckwith

Sometimes I find myself waiting for the opportunities I long for to find *me*. I have some distorted and magical expectation that from out of the mist will appear some individual, or group of individuals, who will make my dreams happen *for* me. I am not out creating opportunities for myself, but waiting in the wings for them to come to me, and feeling discouraged and disappointed when they do not come.

I have to be my own advocate. I have to put myself out there and say, Here I am and this is what I have to offer. Who will be lucky enough to participate in my adventure? It's for me to choose who's right to help me fulfill my creative vision, and not the other way around. We have the dreams and inclinations that we have for a good reason. But they serve no purpose at all unless we have the courage and the perseverance to move steadily toward them.

I take some small action each day in the direction
of my dreams. I understand that it is up to me
to create opportunities for success in my life.

December 3

It's so hard when I have to, and so easy when I want to.
—ANNIE GOTTLIER

If we want to be successful at changing our bad habits, we have to do more than push up against them with disciplined resistance. We have to learn to make the choice *for* the change we want rather than *against* the old behavior. We have to steer ourselves in a positive direction. Otherwise, we set ourselves up for failure. It's not about what we *can't* do anymore and poor us. It's about what we *can* do if we make the change.

We are all following trails of crumbs to some destination or another. We can follow them to fulfillment and happiness or we can follow them to spiritual imprisonment and desperation. Let's be honest about what direction we're moving in and carefully consider our next step, and the one after that. Where are we headed, and what do we choose?

Instead of running away from the things I don't want,
I change my perspective and learn how to move
steadily in a positive direction.

December 4

Here is the world. Beautiful and terrible things will happen.
Don't be afraid.
—FREDERICK BUECHNER

The truth is that we cannot know for sure what will happen with the decisions and choices that we make. We can figure and speculate until we are dizzy from our figuring, and still we can't know. And not knowing can paralyze us because we crave certainty and we are afraid to fail. But the only real failure may be in our not trying things because of our fear. Some of the things we try are bound to result in better outcomes than others, but they all lead us somewhere, and even if we fall flat, we learn *something*.

Let's take risks and be willing to see how things turn out. It's useless to tell ourselves that we should have known better. How could we have known? The only way to know is to try. So let's give our considered inclinations a chance and be gentle with ourselves if they don't turn out exactly the way we hope. They always turn out somehow, and we continue to grow.

> *I am willing to try things, and it's okay*
> *if everything I try is not a raging success.*

December 5

Sometimes thinking too much can destroy your momentum.
—Tom Watson

Momentum is an important force in our lives, and it's worth considering how we might use it to our advantage and how we let it work against us. So often we start things with enthusiasm. We build our momentum with great effort and then fizzle out and feel irritated and confused. We stop and turn our attention elsewhere, and we wonder what happened.

Let's learn from trains. They slow down while going up hills and through neighborhoods, but they don't stop. They keep on moving and clanking and rattling down the tracks until they get to wherever they're going. And when they get there, they unload and rest before they carry on.

I conserve my energy resources and maintain steady momentum throughout the day rather than ramping up with too much eagerness and then burning out before the day is done.

December 6

Unless someone like you cares a whole awful lot,
nothing is going to get better. It's not.
—Dr. Seuss

Some people in helping professions are not particularly helpful. There are restaurant servers who seem annoyed when we ask them for things. And then there is the whole breed of customer service representatives whom we encounter by phone. They tell us things that make no sense at all. There is inefficiency and insanity throughout the service industry.

Let's celebrate those who help us without an attitude, and those who have a high level of integrity. Let's recognize their positive approach and genuine desire to be helpful, and thank them for their service. And let's take it a step further and consider how helpful we are with those who seek out *our* guidance. Are we visibly exasperated because we don't want to be bothered? Or do we do better than that?

I am willing to be helpful to others and to treat them
with respect and consideration, even if I'm tired and even if
it's not exactly the way I would have chosen to spend my time.

December 7

*There is more refreshment and stimulation in a nap,
even of the briefest, than in all the alcohol ever distilled.*
—Edward Lucas

I believe in keeping momentum, but I also believe in the power of power naps. They are soothing, restorative, and good for the soul. They are a small indulgence in a world full of trials and effort. Overdone, they result in grogginess and difficulty getting moving again, but closing my eyes for a half an hour or less is often just the thing to get me ready for the next adventure. It's a respite and a cozy quietude. Add some goose down to cover me light and warm, and a short nap is positively heaven on earth. I awaken bright-eyed.

If I am dragging and sleepy, I stop everything and take ten minutes to close my eyes. It's a mini-vacation from the challenges of my day, and the best kind of soul food.

December 8

When the grass looks greener on the other side of the fence,
it may be that they take better care of it there.
—CECIL SELIG

We are sure that we would feel better if only … if only we had a different job, a different house, more money, fewer responsibilities; if we were thinner, stronger, smarter, more tech-savvy… In short, if we were almost *anything* other than what we are, we would feel better. We're sure of it. But the truth is, if we can't be happy *as* we are, *where* we are, chances are we can't be happy anywhere else, either.

There will always be the other side of the fence, where things look better. But our answers and satisfaction are not "over there." And our wholeness is not something to be chased after, but something to be claimed. The grass is not greener on the other side of the fence. It only appears that way to us when we have lost our ability to recognize the beauty and the blessing of what lies right beneath our feet.

I let go of "if only" thoughts and appreciate the blessings
that are already present in my life.

December 9

God is good, but never dance in a small boat.
—IRISH SAYING

We always think we are so wise "at the time," but looking back on happenings in our life makes us realize how naive we really were, and how often we were actually nothing more than shark bait. There is benefit to being on guard when faced with unknown people and situations. I used to trust everyone and everything, puppy-like, and I was easily crushed and frequently hurt.

But I have learned to stand back some in life. Instead of dashing forward with reckless enthusiasm, I have learned to watch for red flags, and to feel for them in my gut. I know now to pay close attention to the unseen and the unspoken. We live in a world of heartache and danger as well as love, and just because I have good intentions does not mean that everyone else does. I have learned to be quiet and observant in unfamiliar territory, and it has saved me from sure disaster more than once. I have learned how to wait and see.

I proceed into the unknown thoughtfully and with caution.

December 10

Long-term happiness is not the by-product of short-term gratification.
—KAREN CASEY

We are all looking for the easy way out and a quick fix. No matter how long it has taken us to become wounded, broken, habitually unhealthy, chronically isolated, or afraid of life, we figure, almost instinctively, that once we make a decision that we want things to be different, that it should just *happen* for us ... with minimal effort and long-lasting results.

But our journey toward the light is often as arduous and lengthy as our descent has been. We make progress little by little, and never as fast as we want to. Frequently, we throw in the towel and revert to our old style of being and living, righteously and with exasperation: "It's been *two weeks* and nothing's happened. It's useless. Why should I bother? Things will never change." But they will change and they do, slowly, over time. We feel as if we are getting nowhere, but if we keep at it, we will make the complete loop and learn to live differently at last.

> ***Change in my life results from the daily attention***
> ***I am willing to give it.***

December 11

Love is the only sane and satisfactory answer
to the problem of human existence.
—ERICH FROMM

Love is the answer to all that plagues us: not the idealized, romantic kind of love, not physical passion or mental obsession, but a gentle generosity of the spirit, a simple happiness, and an approach to life and to people that is appreciative and willing to understand. If we are not living by the light of love, then we are blocked to it somehow and experiencing darkness instead. It is then that we travel the lonely road of fear, judgment, and isolation.

To help others helps us. There is no greater joy than the joy of giving. It's as simple as reaching out just a little and letting someone know that we are paying attention and we care.

Loving grows love, and if we give it, we get it. We feel it. We fill up with it. It is the answer to all of our angst and worry and selfish frustration, and ultimately, I believe, it the reason for our being here at all.

I generously express my love.

December 12

Fall seven times. Stand up eight.
—Japanese proverb

When I am made to wait when waiting is the last thing I have time for, the question is, how do I handle it? And the answer is, sometimes better than at other times. I imagine we can all deal fairly easily with one small inconvenience, or maybe two in a row. But three is pushing it, and anything beyond that starts to get into the neighborhood of dark humor. It's either a cruel trick or a clever lesson that we are forced to slow down when we have the least amount of time to spare. The only possible response at that point, assuming walking away is not an option, is to explode in rage, tears, or laughter. Let's learn to laugh more and rage less, not only with waiting when we don't want to, but with the whole range of curveballs that life throws our way.

I am willing to laugh when life
throws unexpected roadblocks in my path.

December 13

A fine landscape is like a piece of music;
it must be taken at the right tempo.
—PAUL SCOTT

I am a strident walker. I walk with purpose and what almost feels like urgency. My steps are tense and quick, rapid-fire. I move through space with strength and determination. There's nothing relaxed or quiet about it. I'm sure that anyone watching me walk must think I'm in a hurry, whether I am or not. And I'm not the only one. Lots of us walk that way. Maybe it's our culture. We are always trying to get so much done.

Older people, and children, move more slowly. They are more about strolling than striding, and perhaps they are the wiser for it. They don't see what the big rush is. They want to rest for a moment, or stop and look at the caterpillar on the side of the path, or remember something from fifty years ago that this moment reminds them of, or feel the sun on their face. And when they decide to pick up the tempo, they pick it up out of joy rather than intensity. Sometimes children just *have to* hop and skip down the road.

I relax the way I walk. I don't have to live life in a rush.

December 14

Everybody needs beauty as well as bread.
—JOHN MUIR

It's not only our stomachs that get hungry, but our eyes, and our hands, and our skin and hearts. We are hungry for beauty, for touch, for love, for good smells and fresh air in our lungs. So we must learn, daily, to feed ourselves.

If we notice the details of our lives and appreciate small things, we need never feel hungry or lost or malnourished. We can feel grateful instead, for so much deliciousness all around us, and that we are blessed with an endless free supply … if we only pay attention. We can learn to nourish our hearts and all of our senses, and if the truth be told, it's our responsibility, and no one else's, to do just that.

I bring awareness to beauty and delicious smells and good music and warm hugs. I allow my senses to be fed indulgently every day, and understand that I needn't feel hungry if I pay attention and express appreciation for the sensual details of my daily life.

December 15

Christmas waves a magic wand over this world, and behold,
everything is softer and more beautiful
—NORMAN VINCENT PEALE

I used to feel irritated by Christmas, by the music coming too early and the commercialism of it and the crowds and all of my self-imposed have-tos. I didn't want to disappoint anyone, so I overdid on every front. But as my children have grown, and I have grown up a bit myself, I have learned to welcome the soft beauty of Christmas, and to feel the festivity of the music and lights and decorations, without any of the old pressure.

If I slow down enough to feel and appreciate it, this is a magical time of year. And what we are celebrating, after all, is the birth of love and forgiveness in our world. What joy in that! It's a sensational feast every day of the month. Christmas is not just a day, it's a season. Let's be joyful and playful and patient and appreciative for the whole thing! Let's not miss any of it due to pressure or angst. Let's go with the flow and enjoy every bit of the ride.

I feel the spirit of Christmas within me,
and I am filled up with love.

December 16

What I take from my nights, I add to my days.
—LEON DE ROTROU

Loving someone is not all rose petals and rainbows. When we are hurting, or the one we love is hurting, there is a brutality to the rawness of emotion that simply doesn't exist with run-of-the-mill others. The love connection we feel becomes exactly the thing that makes us ache. We share each other's pain, just as we share each other's joy on better days. Maybe as much as anything, love is caring enough about someone to be willing to go through anything with them, to share it all, the whole ride.

Even during the worst pain, there are moments of relief, of quiet, a ray of sun shining through the window. And it seems like it will never end, will never be better, will never be right again, but it will end and it will get better. It always does. We have to hang in and hold on and wait and breathe and love with all of our hearts. Hurt and pain are a part of the journey. When they show up, that's when we need to love each other the most.

Sometimes the most difficult situations
bring the greatest blessings in the end.

354

December 17

Ride the energy of your own unique spirit.
—GABRIELLE ROTH

It is our flaws and our errors and our human vulnerability that make us beautiful. When we acknowledge and accept our limitations with good humor and a sense of grace, then we are good company to be around. But if we pretend to be better than we are, if we pretend to be richer or smarter or more secure, then we are hard to take.

Let's be easy in our skin and full of forgiveness and love—for ourselves as well as others. Let's learn to enjoy simple pleasures and be honest about who we are. Let's stop thinking and believing that we need to be more or less of anything and find a way to get comfortable simply to be.

I am just right and completely whole.
I don't have to pretend that I am anything other than what I am.

December 18

Some people go to priests; others to poetry; I to my friends.
—VIRGINIA WOOLF

Don't be afraid to let people in on your life. Share your journey with them. Tell them about your happiness and celebrations, and admit to them when you're struggling. It's inspiring and beautiful to witness how they are willing to rally around and help out when help is needed … in unexpected and delightful ways. What a wonderful, powerful, incredible thing to have a network of good friends! Gather them up and appreciate them dearly. They will carry you through in the end.

I appreciate my friends, and I'm not afraid to ask for help when I need it. As much as I have a need, they have a need to help.

December 19

Man is the only animal that laughs and weeps;
for he is the only animal that is struck with the difference between
what things are and what they ought to be.
—WILLIAM HAZLITT

Being human is hard work, with all of our sensitivities and ailments, our grand emotions, our egos and manipulations, our resentments and tears, our need for sleep and food, and our hunger for love. In some ways, we are a pitiable lot.

But we also have our joy and glory, our sensibilities and laughter and hope. We have potential and fine dining and soft sheets and bodies that move and feel and stretch.

We are a mix of love and fear, of human desperation and high spiritual aims. And maybe, ultimately, it's the mix in us that makes us so wonderful and beautiful. Maybe it's the mix that keeps us going and carries us forth.

I accept and appreciate the mix of me.
I appreciate who I am, and who I am not.

December 20

As we struggle to make sense of things, life looks on in repose.
—Author unknown

I like things resolved. I like them wrapped up and tucked away tight. Oozing discomfort and murky feelings frustrate me. And yet, when that's the way it is, what choice do I have? What choice do any of us have? I am always trying to rush the process. But I am learning, albeit slowly, that I will understand what I need to understand when I need to understand it, and not a minute before. All of my wanting and figuring will not speed things up a bit or bring me any sooner to resolution and peace.

My peace will come when I can learn to be comfortable with uncertainty and the lack of clear sight. Everything happens on time and in perfect order, even if it's not my time and not my idea of order. I can trust that somehow or other it will all make sense in the end.

I don't have to understand what I cannot understand.
Peace will come when I surrender to the unfolding unknown.

December 21

When in doubt, wear red.
—Bill Blass

A friend of mine has a pair of red cowboy boots, and when she wears them, they give her power. She told me so, and I believe her. The way we dress ourselves sets a mood. We can be shlumpy or we can command respect. We can wear what's old, baggy, ratty, or torn. We can dress to impress, dress to seduce, or dress to kill. We can wear what's fitted and crisp, what's fashionable, or what's becoming.

But whatever we wear, we set a tone. We tell the world something about ourselves. So let's wear the clothes that authentically represent our desired state of mind and body. If it's red cowboy boots, let's break them out. Let's not be afraid to express ourselves in cloth and color and texture and design. Let's have fun with it. Let's adorn ourselves with joy!

I think twice before slobbing around town in the same old sweatshirt. I make an effort to look my best so I can feel my best.

December 22

My theory is that men are no more liberated than women.
—Indira Gandhi

For modern men, there seems to be a certain prejudice in reverse. They do everything that women do. They are stay-at-home dads, folders of laundry, caretakers, lovers, friends, and children of aging parents. They suffer from insecurities and fear, from worry and a lack of self-confidence. We are all interested in tips for healthier relationships, and tools for patience, and ways to be kind. But media pieces on such topics largely leave men out by default and by assumption.

Let's change the way we think about men. Let's include them in our emotional journeys if they want to be included, and let them know they are welcome and their input is appreciated. Let's make our quest for richness of the spirit and vital living more about the human heart and less about the female hormone. Let's celebrate the evolved male perspective and honor the magnificent men in our lives!

*I accept and appreciate the sensitivity in men
and their depth of spirit and fullness of heart.*

December 23

Surrender to win.
—AUTHOR UNKNOWN

If something happens that challenges me greatly, I resist it. "Oh no!" I think. "Not this!" I try to ward it off, push it away, or, at the very least, get through it as quickly as I can. I don't want to experience it. I reach for my blinders and all of my numbing tools. I don't like it and I don't want it. "Dear God," I beg, "please take it back!"

And yet, if I surrender to whatever it is, if I say "okay" instead of "oh no," all the tension and strain depart, and I am left open to the strange beauty of hardship. It has its own kind of grace. And I end up blessed by the very thing I was sure had come to curse me.

Instead of raging and resisting,
I am willing to be okay with life as it comes.

December 24

*What is life? It is the flash of a firefly in the night.
It is the breath of a buffalo in the wintertime. It is the little
shadow which runs across the grass and loses itself in the sunset.*
—CROWFOOT

Life is not about my agenda or what makes sense to me. It's not my plan that turns the wheels or drives the ship. It's not what I think that happens, or what I want, or even what I *know*. Life is mysterious. It is a journey of all the things that cannot be anticipated. It is twists and turns and convoluted passages. It is puzzling. It is paradoxical. It is eternal and momentary and none of the above and all of the above.

The purpose of my life is simply to experience the ride—to exalt in the joys and suffer the hardships, to feel the feelings and to share it all with the people I love. That's the whole deal and the real deal: to not make sense of life, or manipulate it, or master it, but simply to live it, however it may come.

I don't have to stress and strain. Life is to celebrate.

December 25

If those who owe us nothing gave us nothing, how poor we would be.
—ANTONIO PORCHIA

It's important for me to pause for a moment and consider the meaning of Christmas, and to clarify my hopes and intentions. I consciously open my heart to let love in. I become willing to receive gracefully and to give without expectations. I invite joy and hospitality and patience and grace into my being. I welcome the songs and the lights and the presents and the good food. I express gratitude for my family, and the people who love me, and for the people I love. I pray for good humor and serenity, and to be an instrument of peace. I vow to let be what is, and to let the day and the week unfold as it will, free from my interference and free from my complaint. I welcome Christmas and the whole range of emotions that it brings. I welcome it absolutely and with joy.

I open my heart and my spirit
to the grateful loving energy of Christmas.

December 26

In seed time learn, in harvest teach, in winter enjoy.
—WILLIAM BLAKE

I have always liked the winter. I like cold, fresh mornings and seeing my breath in foggy clouds. I like walking outdoors and feeling my cheeks sting from the sharp air. I like down jackets and bundling up, and I like the snow. It is soft and quiet and clean. It is thick and heavy or light and fluffy, but magical either way. And I even like cold, wintery rain. Whatever comes this time of year, I like the freshness of it.

As a culture, I think we spend too much time complaining about the winter. "It's so cold!" we moan. And then, before we know it, summer comes around again and we're at odds with the heat and humidity. Let's make an effort to enjoy what's here. Let's enjoy the mysterious changeability of the weather and the sky.

I enjoy the blessings of winter. I have gratitude for the fresh, crisp air, and I welcome the magical snow!

December 27

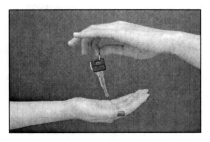

Put down the cross. We need the wood.
—AUTHOR UNKNOWN

I have ridiculously high standards, a desire to help *everyone*, and a built-in struggle ethic. And I am also discovering that I approach whatever is new in my life with a certain amount of apprehension, because I am sure it will somehow end up being more work for me in the end, and it might just tip me over the edge. I look at opportunity and see it as a chore and a burden. I don't seem to welcome all the wonderful things that *could* happen. Instead, I feel put upon in advance.

Perhaps I expect life to stretch me to my outside limit because that is how far I habitually stretch myself. I live in a kind of maxed-out state, just barely making it from one day to the next. I *could* choose to *not* do, and delegate more, and ask for help, and take a break when I need one. It's up to me. If I want to allow room for wonderful new things to enter my life, all it takes is my willingness.

> *If I feel like a martyr, then I must be one,*
> *and it's up to me to ease up and back off.*

December 28

Children make your life important.
—ERMA BOMBECK

I am grateful for my children. They have taught me courage, patience, resilience, and unconditional love. They have pushed my limits, stretched my heartstrings, and impressed me over and over with their unique gifts. They have inspired me with their incredible twin connection, and shown me what it is to have that kind of sibling by your side. Sienna is all heart and ferocity, and Nick is charisma and grace. They rise. They fall. They struggle. They yearn. They push into the world for success and independence and come home for love and hugs.

It's their birthday today. Their being here has changed everything.

I love my children with all of my heart.

December 29

It takes courage to grow up and become who you really are.
—E. E. CUMMINGS

It is a great gift to be without pretense; to be genuine, human, and fallible; to be able to laugh at ourselves. It is attractive and desirable to be authentic and to live without apology. Self-consciousness comes so easily. We are awkward and unsure. We keep adjusting our clothing and fixing our hair. And in so doing, we draw attention to our uneasiness, and we do not inspire confidence, not in ourselves or others.

When we feel good about ourselves, other people like to be around us, because we give them permission to feel good, too. Authenticity is like the open air. It is spacious and allowing. So let's not worry about being perfect, just for today. Let's not try to impress anyone. Let's just relax and enjoy the feeling of being who we are exactly where we are. Behaving in such a manner attracts good things to us, and appreciative people. There is nothing quite like the energy of simple happiness. Let's allow it in our lives.

> *I leave self-consciousness behind*
> *and let myself be myself, exactly as I am.*

December 30

*Using the power of decision gives you the capacity to get past
any excuse to change any and every part of your life in an instant.*
—ANTHONY ROBBINS

No matter how choiceless we feel, no matter how indebted or
trapped or tied down, we are never stuck. We choose our lives
every day, and at any time we can choose differently. We choose
to be accountable, or not to be. We feel as if our situations are
so binding and sticky and permanent. And yet, in a moment, everything can change. A decision or an accident or a difference of
opinion can alter our whole life's direction. What we do with our
lives is up to us.

So the next time we find ourselves complaining, let's remember how we got where we are, and if we don't like it, let's make
the decision to change. It's nothing but fear that holds us back,
and fear is more a shadow than a reality. It always appears bigger
than it is. It's better to take a chance at living a life of authentic
happiness than to settle for moaning and complaining through
our days and pretending that we have no other options.

*I stop complaining about the way things are
and make changes where changes can be made.*

December 31

In the Middle Ages, they had guillotines, stretch racks,
whips and chains. Nowadays, we have a much more effective
torture device called the bathroom scale.
—STEPHEN PHILLIPS

Occasionally I encounter people who have taken their weight loss program too far. They are past trim and have become emaciated and sunken. They are depleted, but oh so proud! As a culture, we have misplaced our intuitive ability to feed ourselves. Everything we see and hear in the media reinforces our own insecurity and tells us we can't be trusted to eat good foods in right-sized portions. We think we have to be regulated and restricted and watched like a hawk.

There is so much insanity surrounding our food consumption and body image. Let's make an effort to get happy with our bodies and to pay attention when we eat so that we enjoy our food but know when we have had enough. Let's find a way to be okay with a little bit of fat. Our ideal is unnatural and entirely skewed.

I eat reasonably and do not obsess about food in either direction.
It's okay to be the way I am.

$\mathcal{I}$ndex

B

C

J

JOY: March 22, August 14, August 29, October 3, November 4, November 27, December 15

JOURNEY: September 9, September 25, December 10, December 16

JUDGMENT: February 5, February 15, July 11, November 2

JUST RIGHT: September 3

K

KINDNESS: January 26, February 4, March 7, April 25, May 10, June 23, July 1, July 30, November 23

L

LABELS: August 8

LESSONS: January 23, February 10, August 3, December 4

LETTING GO: January 14, January 20, January 22, January 31, February 26, March 7, March 13, March 14, March 20, March 31, May 30, June 2, June 11, June 13, July 16, September 3, October 31, December 8

LIGHT: June 4, August 17, November 11

LIMITS: October 22

LISTENING: June 17, August 20

LOVE: January 18, February 14, February 18, February 20, February 25, March 11, April 4, May 12, May 21, June 7, June 20, July 16, August 31, September 3, October 13, October 15, December 11, December 16, December 25, December 28

P

PROJECTION: March 5, May 13, June 6, June 9, September 9, November 20

R

REACTIVE: February 1

RECEIVING: December 25

RELAXATION: February 28, June 30, July 6, July 23, August 24, December 13

RELEASE: January 29

RESENTMENT: January 23

RESISTANCE: April 7, May 1, May 29, July 29, August 23, October 5, December 23

RESPONSIVE: February 1

RESOLUTION: August 26

REST: December 7

RESTORATION: July 26

RHYTHM: August 24, August 27, November 4

ROUTINES: July 19, October 23

RUSHING: November 13, December 13

S

SADNESS: February 25, August 27

SAFETY: July 27, October 7, December 9

SARCASM: November 18

SAYING NO: March 1

SECRETS: January 24, February 13, February 27

Photo Credits

Photos on pages 126 and 187 by David Beecy.

Photos on pages 11, 16, 22, 37, 41, 52, 96, 109, 119, 128, 140, 189, 232, 295, and 321 by Kimberly Berlin.

Photos on pages 19, 32, 56, 87, 92, 99, 144, 151, 153, 164, 177, 195, 238, 276, 288, 292, 300, 302, 311, 312, 323, 340, 358, and 368 by Jeff Bingham.

Photo on page 215 by Kyli Blattner.

Photos on pages 320 and 330 by Patty Buchholz.

Photos on pages 77, 82, 197, 221, 242, 253, 274, 289, and 303 by Donna Burch-Brown.

Photo on page 310 by Erika Carry.

Photos on pages 15, 23, 44, 196, 210, and 361 by Stephen Dombrosk.

Photos on pages 7, 33, 76, 98, 100, 101, 114, 122, 124, 130, 154, 158, 173, 176, 181, 209, 225, 233, 237, 266, 273, 278, 317, 329, 338, 341, and 357 by Mike Florio.

Photo on page 178 by Kyle Gordon.

Photos on pages 6 and 175 by Gruff S. Herrman.

Photos on pages 4, 5, 8, 12, 13, 14, 20, 26, 28, 30, 36, 38, 48, 49, 50, 53, 55, 57, 64, 69, 72, 73, 75, 79, 81, 83, 84, 85, 86, 89, 90, 93, 94, 103, 104, 105, 106, 107, 108, 111, 112, 115, 117, 118, 120, 127, 129, 132, 136, 137, 138, 141, 145, 147, 148, 150, 155, 156, 159, 160, 162, 163, 165, 166, 167, 169, 170, 171, 179, 182, 183, 185, 190, 192, 198, 200, 201, 202, 203, 204, 205, 206, 207, 208, 211, 213, 214, 217, 218, 219, 222, 223, 224, 226, 227, 229, 230, 235, 236, 240, 244, 245, 246, 248, 250, 251, 252, 254, 255,

256, 257, 258, 259, 260, 261, 262, 264, 265, 268, 269, 270, 271,
272, 275, 279, 280, 282, 283, 284, 287, 290, 293, 296, 299, 304,
305, 306, 308, 309, 313, 314, 315, 322, 324, 325, 326, 327, 332,
333, 334, 335, 337, 339, 342, 343, 346, 355, 356, 359, 360, 362,
363, 366, 367, and 369 by Nathalie Herrman.

Photos on pages 18, 25, 40, 42, 51, 54, 58, 61, 67, 68, 113, 135,
143, 168, 172, 174, 186, 231, 243, 263, 285, 291, 318, 328, 336,
344, 347, 348, 353, 354, and 365 by Ellen Lawson.

Photos on pages 298 and 349 by Llewellyn Worldwide Ltd.

Photos on pages 9, 17, 24, 27, 34, 45, 47, 71, 121, 188, 194, 249,
301, and 352 by Lynne Menturweck.

Photos on pages 80, 110, 152, 239, and 297 by Andrea Neff.

Photos on pages 29, 35, 70, 78, 102, 116, 142, 286, and 307 by Lisa
Novak.

Photo on page 345 by Lynda Ose.

Photos on pages 228 and 277 by Marv Raiola.

Photos on pages 21, 39, 43, 59, 65, 91, 95, 125, 131, 133, 146,
157, 161, 180, 193, 241, 267, 294, 331, 350, and 351 by Stuart
Rakoff.

Photos on pages 191 and 216 by Holly Roth.

Photos on pages 46 and 97 by Kathy Schneider.

Photo on page 220 by Nick Turecamo.

Photo on page 139 by Robert Turecamo.

Photo on page 319 by Sienna Turecamo.

Photos on pages 123 and 199 by Cleberson Veiga.

Photos on pages 60, 63, 134, 212, and 364 by
Angela Wix.

Photo on page 74 by Amy Wynne.

Photos on pages 31 and 234 by Connie Zebro.

Photo on page 88 by Ken Zebro.

Photos on pages 10, 62, 66, 149, and 316 by Ruthie Zebro.

Photos on pages 184, 247, and 281 by Barb Zicari.

To Write to the Author

If you wish to contact the author or would like more information about this book, please write to the author in care of Llewellyn Worldwide Ltd. and we will forward your request. Both the author and publisher appreciate hearing from you and learning of your enjoyment of this book and how it has helped you. Llewellyn Worldwide Ltd. cannot guarantee that every letter written to the author can be answered, but all will be forwarded. Please write to:

Nathalie W. Herrman
℅ Llewellyn Worldwide
2143 Wooddale Drive
Woodbury, MN 55125-2989

Please enclose a self-addressed stamped envelope for reply,
or $1.00 to cover costs. If outside the U.S.A., enclose
an international postal reply coupon.

Many of Llewellyn's authors have websites with additional information and resources. For more information, please visit our website at http://www.llewellyn.com

GET MORE AT **LLEWELLYN.COM**

Visit us online to browse hundreds of our books and decks, plus sign up to receive our e-newsletters and exclusive online offers.

- **Free tarot readings • Spell-a-Day • Moon phases**
- **Recipes, spells, and tips • Blogs • Encyclopedia**
- **Author interviews, articles, and upcoming events**

GET SOCIAL WITH **LLEWELLYN**

Find us on
Facebook

www.Facebook.com/LlewellynBooks

Follow us on

www.Twitter.com/Llewellynbooks

GET BOOKS AT **LLEWELLYN**

LLEWELLYN ORDERING INFORMATION

Order online: Visit our website at www.llewellyn.com to select your books and place an order on our secure server.

Order by phone:
- Call toll free within the U.S. at 1-877-NEW-WRLD (1-877-639-9753)
- Call toll free within Canada at 1-866-NEW-WRLD (1-866-639-9753)
- We accept VISA, MasterCard, and American Express

Order by mail:
Send the full price of your order (MN residents add 6.875% sales tax) in U.S. funds, plus postage and handling to: Llewellyn Worldwide, 2143 Wooddale Drive Woodbury, MN 55125-2989

Melissa Alvarez

365 WAYS

to **RAISE** *Your*

FREQUENCY

SIMPLE TOOLS TO INCREASE
YOUR SPIRITUAL ENERGY
FOR BALANCE, PURPOSE, AND JOY

365 Ways to Raise Your Frequency

Simple Tools to Increase Your Spiritual Energy for Balance, Purpose, and Joy

MELISSA ALVAREZ

The soul's vibrational rate, our spiritual frequency, has a huge impact on our lives. As it increases, so does our capacity to calm the mind, connect with angels and spirit guides, find joy and enlightenment, and achieve what we want in life.

This simple and inspiring guide makes it easy to elevate your spiritual frequency every day. Choose from a variety of ordinary activities, such as singing and cooking. Practice visualization exercises and techniques for reducing negativity, manifesting abundance, tapping into Universal Energy, and connecting with your higher self. Discover how generous actions and a positive attitude can make a difference. You'll also find long-term projects and guidance for boosting your spiritual energy to new heights over a lifetime.

978-0-7387-2740-0, 432 pp., 5 x 7　　　　　　　**$16.95**

To order, call 1-877-NEW-WRLD
Prices subject to change without notice
Order at Llewellyn.com 24 hours a day, 7 days a week!

CPSIA information can be obtained at www.ICGtesting.com
Printed in the USA
LVOW10s0721101215

465776LV00008B/8/P